T0318145

charlotte perriand

the modern life

edited by justin mcguirk

**the
DESIGN
MUSEUM**

On 24 October 1996, Charlotte Perriand celebrated her ninety-third birthday in London at the Design Museum. It coincided with the opening day of her first museum show in the UK, one that presented her as 'a Modernist Pioneer'. She had spent the previous week in the galleries overseeing the installation of the exhibition, by all accounts both hands-on and on her feet for hours at a time, clad in a pair of striking pink Nike trainers. Design Museum director Paul Thompson recalls her giving detailed instructions to two near-herniated technicians as they staggered around with one of the large Maison de la Tunisie book-shelving units, moving it around until it was just right, and then Perriand herself twisting her celebrated *Chaise longue basculante* a few millimetres this way and that until she was happy with where it sat in the gallery space.

Her attention to detail was lifelong, as was her belief in integrated 'ambience' and the notion of 'equipping' a space rather than decorating it, what she described in 1996 as 'the resonance of things together'. She was indeed a modernist pioneer, but she evolved her approach throughout a creative life that began in the late 1920s and ended in 1999, from the machine aesthetic to a more sensual engagement with the natural world. 'A concept can be affirmed in different ways,' as she put it, 'depending on place, materials, technique and traditions.'[1]

This exhibition in London seeks to re-explore Charlotte Perriand twenty-five years on. It evolved partly out of the research and work done for the monumental exhibition staged in Paris at the Fondation Louis Vuitton in 2019, and I'd like to thank Jean-Paul Claverie and curator Sébastien Cherruet for their collegiality and support. That exhibition affirmed Perriand as one of the great collaborators and synthesisers in the history of design, a woman who was able to work creatively alongside (and sometimes under the shadow of) Le Corbusier, Jean Prouvé and Pierre Jeanneret, Picasso and Léger too, but whose own singular achievements are now finally being recognised. In that spirit, we have invited the architecture collective Assemble and graphic design studio A Practice for Everyday Life to design the exhibition, with an attention to detail and sensitivity to 'the resonance of things together' of which Perriand would have been proud.

We are also exploring Perriand's creative processes as never before, exhibiting numerous previously unseen drawings and giving the opportunity for the viewer, and – we hope – for contemporary designers and architects to look closely at the way she thought and worked. The Archives Charlotte Perriand have been incredibly generous with loans and research, and I'd like to pay a personal tribute to Pernette Perriand and Jacques Barsac for their boundless support, advice and enthusiasm.

After the Design Museum exhibition had opened, towards the end of 1996, Charlotte Perriand was interviewed by the *New York Times*. She was asked about her work in relationship to history, particularly the constraints of modernism and the anxiety around the rampant use of historicist pastiche in postmodernism. She replied,

> I agree it is necessary to be acquainted with everything that has gone before us, and I respect each era and all that it can express. But I think of tradition as a chain, with the last link being the previous century. And to that link, we attach another that we make ourselves, from the century in which we live.[2]

Even in looking back, she never turned her back on the future, which is one of the reasons there is still so much to learn from looking closely at Charlotte Perriand again today.

Tim Marlow
Chief Executive and Director of the Design Museum

1   Charlotte Perriand, *A Life of Creation*
     (New York: Monacelli Press, 2003), 70.
2   Holly Brubach, 'The Rediscovered Modernist',
     New York Times (15 December 1996), 53.

justin mcguirk

introduction

Charlotte Perriand, who was born in 1903 and passed away in 1999, lived a life that spanned the twentieth century. Hers was a modern life almost by default. But it was also searchingly and proactively modern, the life of someone committed to being of her time. Of course, if one were to interrogate any of these statements, one would have to define 'modern'. But what might be more interesting is to ask whether there was such a thing as *the* modern life. And, if so, to what extent did Perriand's work as a designer help define what that means. This is not to suggest that there is a simple definition but that, on the contrary, Perriand's long career charts the dog-legs and U-turns of modernism itself, from the machine aesthetic to organic forms, from industry to craftsmanship to a settled position between the two. In her attitudes to furniture, domestic space, mass housing, the kitchen and leisure,

her work pursues modernist ambitions, and embodies modernist compromises and contradictions. At the same time, her own life – in its free-spiritedness, in its highly conscious balance of work, leisure and sport – was quintessentially modern. And yet the artfulness with which she lived was also uniquely hers. It was a philosophy of sorts, and that, too, is something that we shall explore.

Though trained in the decorative arts tradition, Perriand emerged a fully formed modernist at just twenty-four when she exhibited her own apartment at the Salon d'Automne of 1927. A well-known photograph of her in that apartment on Place Saint-Sulpice captures the young woman with a gamine haircut, a bold-print dress and a necklace of industrial ball bearings – the very picture of the modern woman, wearing a symbol of the Machine Age

Charlotte Perriand and Marianne Clouzot in Entre-deux-Eaux in the Alps, August 1932

'Rangement', *Techniques et Architecture* (August 1950)

around her neck. The furniture she designed for her own home secured her entry into the studio of Le Corbusier, where she spent a formative decade whose lessons and friendships would shape the rest of her career. Even if the principles were Corbu's, it was Perriand who was the driving force behind the furniture the studio showed at the Salon d'Automne in 1929. The *Chaise longue basculante*, the *Fauteuil grand confort* and the *Siège à dossier basculant* quickly entered the canon of early modernist furniture, and continue to serve as symbols of what was an avant-garde assault on the home.

One tenet that Perriand took away from her time with Corbu and Pierre Jeanneret at the rue de Sèvres was the idea that furniture was 'equipment'. Despite the overtones of functionalist efficiency, Perriand's *équipement* was elegant and, as Tim Benton notes in this book, rather more comfortable than the epochal chairs by the master of tubular steel, Marcel Breuer. While her aesthetic sensibility evolved, that practical notion of equipping a space as part of an integrated spatial plan – as opposed to decorating it – remained central to her thinking. There, already, you have one definition of 'the modern'. But through her connection to Corbu and Jeanneret, Perriand was steeped in the modernism of the 1920s and 30s. She attended the famous meeting of the Congrès internationaux d'architecture moderne (CIAM) in Athens in 1933 and imbibed its sense of architecture's social purpose. In response to the second CIAM conference in 1929, she had designed a minimum dwelling, *la céllule*, aimed at low-income families, in which each individual had a space of fourteen square metres (150 square feet). The rigour of designing to such constraints, and the ambition to touch the lives of the average citizen – and not just the elite clientele that could afford a chaise longue – shaped her practice right to the end.

These were the years of Perriand's dogmatic modernism, if you will. Her 1929 essay 'Wood or Metal?' speaks the language of revolution, proclaiming the 'AESTHETICS OF METAL'

and the virtues of the 'NEW MAN'. These were not just aesthetic convictions. She maintained a firm belief, as she later wrote to Jeanneret, that 'Architecture' meant 'working for mankind'.[1] As we shall see, she softened her position on materials, but she retained her egalitarian principles. In the 1930s, she did her best to keep abreast of socialist thinking. She joined courses at the Workers' University but was aware she stuck out as a *bourgeoise*, and she made two trips to Moscow where her experience of 'actually existing communism' rather dented her idealism. However, where her political convictions found their truest form was in a commitment to democratic design. In the leftist review *Vendredi*, she published designs for storage units that people could get a carpenter to make much more cheaply than the over-decorated sideboards available in the Faubourg Saint-Antoine – here she anticipated Enzo Mari's self-build furniture forty years later. Similarly, her design for a weekend house in 1935 was one that didn't need an architect – 'anyone could put it up' in her view.

As a prominent member of the Union des artistes modernes (UAM), in 1949 she helped stage the exhibition *Formes Utiles*, where she was instrumental in including affordable and readily available objects, from baskets and saucepans to light switches, as examples of good design. This was France's equivalent to other, admittedly rather didactic, exhibitions that sought to educate the public in the beauty of utility, such as Max Bill's *Die gute Form* in Switzerland (also 1949) and the *Good Design* exhibitions held at the Museum of Modern Art in New York in the 1940s and 50s. When the UAM disbanded nine years later, it was with a sense that its mission was largely accomplished.

Recalling *Formes Utiles*, Perriand wrote in her autobiography, 'There is art in everything, whether it be an action, a vase, a saucepan, a glass, a piece of sculpture, a jewel, a way of being.'[2] And here one gets a little closer to what was distinct about Perriand's worldview. This is not a loose use of the term 'art', not a mere figure of speech, but an attitude to her work and life that was deliberate and that strove to bring different influences together in a coherent unity. In 1950, she edited a special edition of the magazine *Techniques et Architecture* that she titled *L'art d'habiter* – the art of dwelling. In a manifesto of sorts, she laid out her positions on the design of domestic space, drawing heavily on the years she spent in Japan during the Second World War. Crucially, she began to distinguish herself from the functionalism of the modernist interior in search of something with more soul. *L'art d'habiter* dispatched the dreaded 'decoration' and offered principles that were more spatial and philosophical. Her twin poles, if this is not too reductive, were the Corbusian tenets of architecture and Kakuzō Okakura's *Book of Tea*, which advocated the virtues of simplicity, harmony and emptiness.

Perriand was drawn to numerous aspects of traditional Japanese living – dare one use the term 'lifestyle'? – from open, flexible interiors to the culture of bathing. And one should note that the harmony she sought both in her design and her life was one geared to the needs of the body as much as the home: sunlight, fresh air, views of nature, exercise, the rituals of washing. But the aspect of Okakura's teaism that she

took most seriously was his notion of the vacuum, a necessary emptiness that enables one to focus on what is essential. For Perriand, that emptiness was a quality of space but also an attitude to the things one keeps around. 'Better to spend a day in the sun than to spend it dusting our useless objects,' she wrote in *L'art d'habiter*. And, as banal as it may sound, the pillar of Perriand's art of dwelling was storage. 'What is the most important element in the domestic equipment? We answer unequivocally: storage. Without well-planned storage, empty space in the home becomes impossible.'

It is no coincidence that some of Perriand's most famous pieces are the *bibliothèques* she designed for manufacture by Jean Prouvé's sheet-metal workshop. These room dividers cum storage units – which, ironically, given they were designed for student dormitories, now fetch stratospheric prices at auction – were a means of maintaining spaciousness even in small spaces. For Perriand, storage was 'the vector of order and harmony'.[3] Her preferred approach was architectural. She believed such equipment should be built in, and she advocated architects casting hollow concrete walls for that purpose. With Galerie Steph Simon in the 1950s she developed

Main room on the ground floor of the Méribel chalet, 1960–1

a number of affordable storage systems, using simple plastic drawers, to make order and harmony accessible. Perriand's salutary emptiness had social as well as aesthetic undertones. If modern appliances liberated the housewife from household drudgery, then storage solutions helped liberate the space in which the family lived its life.

Perriand's term for her domestic sensibility was *ambiance*. Ambience, which neatly avoided loaded terms such as 'style' or 'decoration', was a quality expressed in the approach to architectural space, light and the arrangement of a few carefully chosen things. It was about preserving a sense of calm in an increasingly fast-paced world. And, as she pointed out, 'Ambience costs nothing.' Perhaps the place that conveys it most perceptibly is her own chalet in Méribel, a space both rural and sophisticated, a combination of Japanese layout, modernist glazing and the rustic materials of a Savoie peasant house. If prototypical modernist interiors expressed an opening up of volumes and a flattening of surfaces – often with cold, hard materials such as steel and glass – Perriand's mid-career interpretation is softer, warmer and more humane. That has much to do with her ability to reconcile modernist principles with older traditions – such as the Japanese and Savoyard examples mentioned – and with her enduring respect for craftsmanship. And in that delicate balance lies the slippage between modernism as strictly defined and the modern life as Perriand envisaged it.

Later in her life, she moved on from the professional-sounding *l'art d'habiter* to simply *l'art de vivre* – the art of living. This more fluid, more holistic term better evokes Perriand's sensibility, which reflected a life lived on multiple continents and in various modes of action, from the mountains to the sea. She possessed and admired *savoir vivre*. She was a bon vivant, a traveller and a sensualist. And that latter quality is expressed in her

attitude to craft and materials. This is one area in which modernism in general and Perriand in particular compromised on earlier positions – the ideal of mass production was not always possible, nor desirable. For Perriand this turn began in the 1930s. Inspired by the objects she found and photographed on beaches and in forests – and with the machine aesthetic rapidly becoming associated with militarisation – she turned to natural forms and materials. It began pragmatically, when she made a version of her *Siège a dossier basculant* in wood with rush seating for the *Maison du jeune homme* (House for a young man) in 1935. Her fellow modernist Pierre Chareau took her to task for that chair (hadn't she written a manifesto in favour of metal?) but, she wrote in her memoir, 'I quickly understood that barriers and contradictions don't exist as such. A concept can be affirmed in different ways depending on place, materials, techniques and traditions ...'. More than that, she enjoyed this humble chair's sensual qualities. The rounded armrests, carved by a prison inmate,

'called out to be caressed'.[4] Perriand revelled in wood's flesh-like properties. Of the meaty free-form tables she designed in the 1950s, she commented again, 'Wood is made for caressing, and can be soft as a woman's thighs.'[5]

Perriand loved working with craftsmen and felt enriched by their skills. It was not at all unusual for modernist furniture of this period to be made by craftsmen – Glenn Adamson terms this apparent paradox 'handmade modernism' – but what is interesting about Perriand is the way the craftsmanship is left to speak in its true voice. It is never pretending to be industrially made. This is wonderfully evident in the pieces she made with Jean Prouvé's workshop, in the sideboards and built-in storage units. Here, sliding metal doors are sandwiched between curvaceous slabs of wood or graced with fat wooden handles. The *bibliothèques*, too, have that quality of the metalworker collaborating with the carpenter so that it is very clear who did what. Her storage units for Steph Simon were made of wood by her favourite carpenter, Jean Chetaille, and then stacked with injection-moulded plastic drawers. Industry was industry

and craft was craft, and Perriand's ability was in bringing them together in such a way that both were clearly expressed in the finished product.

This was not so much a middle ground as Perriand having her feet firmly planted in both camps. She aspired to mass production and lived an undoubtedly urbane existence, but she also had a deep respect for rural life and craftsmanship. She designed various iterations of a wooden shepherd's stool and would deploy it next to a bookcase of folded sheet-metal and a ceramic by Fernand Léger. This was Perriand's rendition of the modern life, a sensibility – an ambience? – that reconciled contrasting worlds and materials in harmony. This ethos was presented in its fullest form in her exhibition *Proposal for a Synthesis of the Arts* in Tokyo in 1955. Another manifesto, it exemplified her conception of the interior as a holistic continuum of traditional craftsmanship, industrial production and modern art, not to mention a crossroads of Eastern and Western influence. Underpinning the exhibition was her belief, shared with her fellow members of the UAM, that there ought to be no distinction between the so-called decorative and fine arts, or between the mass-produced object and the *objet d'art* – it was all the art of living.

However, there is another respect in which the notion of 'synthesis' is central to Perriand's importance, not just in the history of modernism but in our own times. Can we agree that design is a *synthetic* discipline, one in which the designer brings together the necessary expertise – be it craftspeople, manufacturers or artists – to realise a project? Because Charlotte Perriand was a brilliant synthesiser, by which I mean she was a consummate collaborator. And this, I will argue, is why she remains a crucial role model for the present day.

There are any number of reasons why Perriand's career was once deemed marginal. First, she was a woman, and her primary mode of expression was the interior, a realm largely subsumed under the totalising vision of the male architect. Her early work with Le Corbusier, however much he relied on her, is paradigmatic of that hierarchy. But the other reason is precisely because Perriand was a natural and enthusiastic collaborator. In a number of projects, the ski resort of Les Arcs being the most obvious, she was the driving force but also the connective tissue between her numerous creative partners. And so, in dedicating an exhibition to her work, the key is not to shift the spotlight of the lone genius from Corbu to her, for the lone-genius myth is just that. Rather than claim Perriand as an auteur, the greater value is in presenting her worldview of an integrated approach to design as indistinguishable from her desire to collaborate.

The decade Perriand spent in Le Corbusier's studio established many of the collaborations that would define her career. There was her very close relationship with Pierre Jeanneret, with whom she designed an aluminium mountain shelter, the Refuge Tonneau. There was Junzō Sakakura, who was instrumental in bringing her to Japan and in facilitating her two major

exhibitions there. And there was Corbu himself, with whom, despite a falling out in the late 1930s, she continued to collaborate. She made significant contributions to one of his most canonical projects, the Unité d'habitation. Beyond furnishings and the kitchen unit, she designed architectural programmes such as the arrangement of the mezzanine levels, which comprised a children's area (her idea) alongside a bedroom and bathroom separated by a built-in storage unit.

Perriand also had long-standing collaborations with Fernand Léger and, of course, Jean Prouvé. With Léger she designed the murals for the Ministry of Agriculture pavilion at the 1937 Exposition Internationale des Arts et Techniques – and it was she who brought in the celebrated artist, not the other way around. With Prouvé, the relationship involved not just mutual respect but business interests, as Perriand was drafted in to design products that would make his metalworks in Maxéville more commercially viable. Both were committed to industrial methods of mass production

Living room of the Aiguille Grive residence, Les Arcs, 1986–9. View from the mezzanine

wherever possible, and to the social mission that underlay this approach to modernity. Maxéville was what Perriand liked to call her 'hardware store', the place where she forged the kit of industrial parts that would comprise so many of her storage units, from bookcases and cupboards to sideboards. Prouvé and Perriand were a de facto team – she called them the 'eternal French accomplices'.[6] But Perriand was the catalyst: she brought him in to help with the interiors of a housing block in Brazzaville, Congo; with the design of a proposal for a ski resort in Belleville with the architects Candilis, Josic and Woods; with the furnishings of the Maison de la Tunisie student dormitory in Paris; and ultimately as an advisor on her greatest collaborative project, Les Arcs.

Prouvé and Perriand were friends for nearly six decades and their work together, as often happens with close collaborations, can be difficult to unpick after the fact. The creative streams merge. At Prouvé's retrospective at the Pompidou in 1990, there were pieces of Charlotte's labelled as Jean's. And later, when the market for collectible design started to take off, gallerists were again attributing Charlotte's work to Jean, who was the better known of the two, in hope of raising its value. That particular episode ended in court, with a judge ruling that the work was Perriand's alone. But none of this should distract us from the gift that is the collaborative spirit. Prouvé provided the context – Maxéville – and Perriand used it to create some of her most famous work. We should also not forget that the modular system Perriand designed for the *bibliothèques*, which could be arranged in multiple configurations, made the buyer, too, a collaborator in the finished piece.

In the end, Perriand's legacy is bound up with her integrated approach to design, which necessitated her collaborations. She called it 'architecture–furnishings–environment' – the built and the unbuilt, figure and ground, in a harmonious continuum. What better illustration than Les Arcs, an urban-scale project for tens of thousands of skiers, which nestles into the contours of the mountainside. She may not have been able to call herself an architect, as she hadn't graduated from the École des Beaux Arts, but Les Arcs demonstrates her mastery of architecture–furnishings–environment. In fact, Perriand didn't want to run a practice – 'to hell with the title "architect"' – because she preferred to be independent.[7] And yet she was the creative lead on Les Arcs, a project that would grow at a rate of a thousand units a year. Working with the architect Gaston Regairaz, she established the prototype of the large ski resort. And one can read in her floor plans how uniquely the elements fit together – the way a particular table sits on the plan in relation to the window, the way the room sits in relation to the landscape, the way an interior experience becomes an external envelope. The architect Josep Lluís Sert, who remained friends with Perriand long after their days together at the rue de Sèvres, said of her: 'Perriand creates interiors as an urban planner.'[8]

The last time Perriand had an exhibition at the Design Museum, in 1996, she was concerned at first that she was being presented as a furniture designer. Twenty-five years later, there is no risk of any misunderstanding. Here, she is presented as a synthesiser, a collaborator, an integrator. A Perriand interior remains a kind of ideal, a harmony of contrasts and disciplines, that is difficult to replicate. And it is this ideal that she offered as a framework to those who wished to live a modern life, like her own.

1   Charlotte Perriand, letter to Pierre Jeanneret, 1939. She writes: 'car enfin le Metier d'Architecture c'est travailler pour l'homme, on ne peut travailler pour lui en l'ignorant, et en ignorant toutes les espèces d'hommes qui composent notre pays.'
2   Charlotte Perriand, *A Life of Creation* (New York: Monacelli Press, 2003), 237.
3   Ibid., 31.
4   Ibid., 70.
5   Ibid., 106.
6   Ibid., 290.
7   Ibid., 230.
8   Mary McLeod (ed.), *Charlotte Perriand: An Art of Living* (New York: Harry N. Abrams, 2003), 243.

the machine age

tim benton
jacques barsac

tim benton

the 'furniture adventure' at the rue de sèvres

previous Chrome ball-bearing necklace, 1927
above   Le Corbusier, Charlotte Perriand, Djo-Bourgeois, Jean Fouquet and Percy Scholefield (in back)
        in the Place Saint-Sulpice apartment–studio, 1928

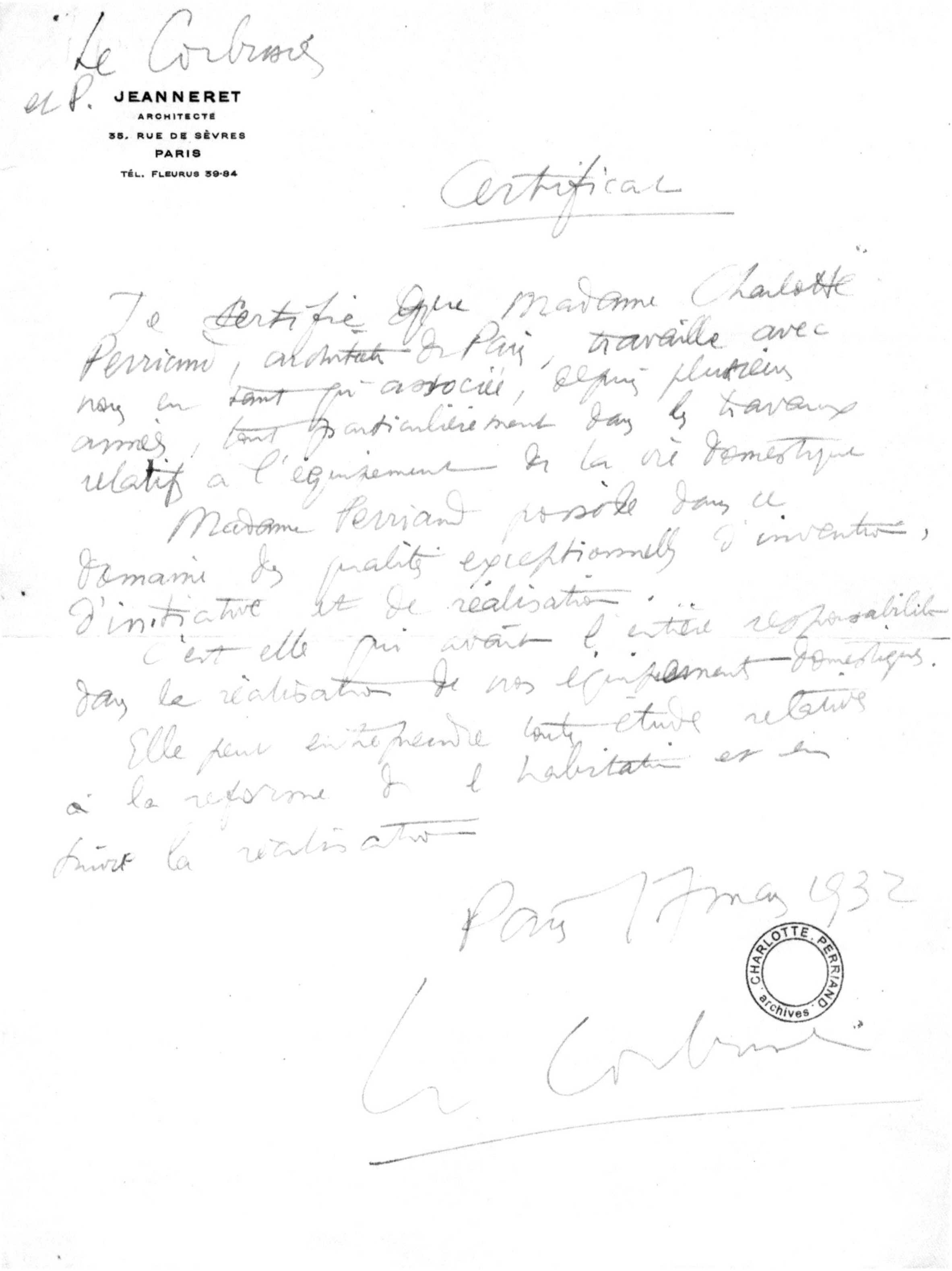

Le Corbusier
et P. **JEANNERET**
ARCHITECTE
35, RUE DE SÈVRES
PARIS
TÉL. FLEURUS 39-84

Certificat

Je certifie que Madame Charlotte Perriand, architecte de Paris, travaille avec nous en tant qu'associé, depuis plusieurs années, tout particulièrement dans les travaux relatif à l'équipement de la vie domestique

Madame Perriand possède dans ce domaine des qualités exceptionnelles d'invention, d'initiative et de réalisation. C'est elle qui avait l'entière responsabilité dans la réalisation de nos équipements domestiques.

Elle peut entreprendre toute étude relative à la réforme de l'habitation et en suivre la réalisation

Paris 17 mars 1932

Le Corbusier

Certificate from Le Corbusier explaining Perriand's role in
the studio as managing domestic 'equipment', 17 March 1932

Two features stand out in Charlotte Perriand's career: her lifelong search for what she called 'the art of living' and a willingness to collaborate with others.[1] As Mary McLeod says, 'she valued simplicity and naturalness and strove for an art of artlessness – one that united play and seriousness, artifice and nature.'[2] Perriand's autobiography, *A Life of Creation*, provides a rich context for her design work, demonstrating her sensitivities to the details of everyday life, her fascination with Japanese aesthetics and customs, and her love of nature and outdoor exercise.[3] She also had a great ability to learn and adapt to new problems, and showed these qualities throughout the first twelve years of her career.

Within eighteen months of graduating from the École de l'Union centrale des arts décoratifs in Paris in 1925, Perriand had become a rising star in the world of Art Deco. Her cabinet for silverware, exhibited in May 1927 at the Salon des artistes décorateurs, was well received. It had been subsidised by the Englishman Percy Scholefield, who became her husband in December of the same year. In two following exhibitions, in October 1927 and 1928, she exhibited two rooms from the studio apartment at 74 rue Bonaparte which they shared. But what might have been a glittering career as an Art Deco designer took a radical turn when Perriand read Le Corbusier's *Vers une architecture* (Toward an Architecture) and, especially, *L'art décoratif d'aujourd'hui* (The Decorative Art of Today). The latter was a root-and-branch attack on the principles and techniques in which she had been trained. Perriand decided that she should work with Le Corbusier. Initially, he rebuffed her advances. But as she moved towards architecture, he was moving back towards design. He had designed furniture before the war and continued to design interiors for his wealthy Swiss clients well into the 1920s. But, with respect to his own architecture, Le Corbusier had followed the advice of the Austrian writer and designer Adolf Loos.[4] Modern man, said Loos, needs no 'modern design' and, above all, no decoration. Leave this to the craftsmen.

Furnish your interiors with the best of what is available. Le Corbusier chose the comfortable leather armchairs made by Maple & Co. or designed by Abel Motté and the cheap, mass-produced bentwood chairs manufactured by Thonet to furnish his houses. Le Corbusier's idea was that most furniture should be built in by the mason, leaving only tables and chairs to be added. Some of his wealthy clients, like Michael and Sarah Stein, refused to submit to these strictures, installing their own antique furniture. Le Corbusier realised that he was going to have to offer his prestigious clients chairs, tables and storage of a certain standing and in a modern style. In particular, he was shocked to see how architects like Mart Stam, Walter Gropius and Mies van de Rohe were using elegant tubular-steel furniture in their interiors. Tubular steel was to furniture what reinforced concrete and steel were to architecture: a means of separating structure from volume and making forms appear weightless. As Perriand wrote in an article in 1930: 'It is a revolution!'[5]

In her *Bar sous le toit* (Bar under the roof) exhibit in the Salon d'Automne in 1927, Perriand used tubular-steel bar stools and created a hovering effect with a card table by deploying chromed sheets of copper that appeared invisible.[6] So, when Le Corbusier visited Perriand's exhibit that October, he realised that she could offer him something he needed – a suite of modern furniture. Perriand quickly settled down to working in the atelier on the rue de Sèvres. One of her first jobs was the gallery in Villa La Roche (1923–5), after two radiators had burst in the winter of 1927. A magnificent table of thick black marble was supported at one end by a block of masonry and at the other by a V-shaped support in tubular steel. This table reproduced the dimensions of Perriand's extendable dining table, installed in her apartment in 1927 and exhibited at the Salon des artistes décorateurs in 1928. The surface of the extendable table was of rubber, supported by a lattice of wooden slats that could expand or contract. The rubber sheet was stored in a large box, passing over a roller that served as a counterweight. She made a second 'luxury' version with a handle that she patented under her married name of Scholefield in 1929.[7] Le Corbusier never adopted this design into the atelier's suite of furniture, and an implied criticism of it can be seen in one of his sketches for the lecture entitled 'L'aventure du mobilier' (The Adventure of Furniture) on 19 October 1929 in Buenos Aires.[8] He argued against the principle of the extendable dining table, a challenge presented to cabinetmakers for centuries, and proposed instead a set of modular tables that could be used around the house but brought together to make a big table for dinner parties. Intriguingly, he added a sketch of Perriand's arrangement of the retractable rubber surface of her extendable table. Presumably, his intention was to argue against unnecessary complication and expense in favour of simple modular units. Perriand would have liked Thonet to manufacture her table, but it never happened.

Perriand soon adopted Le Corbusier's approach to standardised unit construction and her work on the *casiers* (storage cabinets) developed into a lifelong search for convenient, practical and economical solutions. But Perriand was always sensitive to qualities of texture, warmth of materials and effects of touch. Between December 1927 and the summer of 1928, Le Corbusier, Pierre Jeanneret and Perriand created the three chairs that have become classics: the *Chaise longue*, the *Fauteuil grand confort* and the *Fauteuil au dos basculant*, as well as some tables and stools.[9] Perriand designed a swivelling dining chair (the CII Chair), upholstered in red or blue leather, and a set of stools for her own apartment (April–October 1928).[10] Six of these were exhibited in 1928 at the Salon des artistes décorateurs, along with her extendable dining table. These chairs, designed exclusively by her, were incorporated into the suite of furniture attributed to Le Corbusier, Pierre Jeanneret and Perriand.

The dominant idea behind the design of tubular-steel furniture was to create 'types' that could be mass-produced. Simplicity of form and production was combined with the search for a single model that could meet all needs. Le Corbusier and Perriand did not follow this path. The former made a sketch, which he dated 'avril 1927', on which he mused on the wide range of different sitting postures, for relaxing, working, discussing or travelling in a car.[11] His sketch showed nine different sitting postures, divided into men and women.

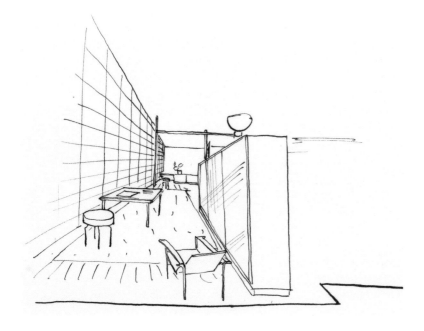

Perspective rendering of 'minimum dwelling' module, 1931

above   Dining room in the Place Saint-Sulpice apartment–studio, as exhibited
         at the Salon des artistes décorateurs, 1928
below   Dining room in the Place Saint-Sulpice apartment–studio, Paris, 1927

He distinguished between two profiles for reclining: one, nearly straight, for men, and one, articulated in an undulating form, which he categorised as female. The latter determined the form of the *Chaise longue*. A similar profile was used in the tiled slab adjoining the sunken bath in the master bedroom of the Villa Savoye. Perriand picked up this idea and took photographs of five wooden mannequins, in different postures, inking in the outlines of her swivel chair, the *Chaise longue*, the *Fauteuil au dos basculant*, the *Grand confort* and a *Siège pliable* (folding chair) of her design that was not constructed until much later.[12] The consequence was that each of the three chairs was completely different from the others. The *Chaise au dos basculant* was a close transcription into steel

of a traditional wooden chair used by the British in the colonies, consisting of a wooden frame and leather straps. The *Fauteuil grand confort* consisted of a cage of tubular steel tubing enclosing upholstered seats and down-filled soft leather cushions. In contrast to the upholstered wooden carcass of the English club armchair, the structure was made visible on the outside. The *Chaise longue* combined the adaptability of the 'Surrepos' reclining divan patented by Dr Pascaud in 1925 (advertised as a 'machine for relaxation') with the simplicity of a Thonet bentwood rocking chair. A patent for the *Chaise longue*, in the name of the three designers, was lodged in April 1929 and granted in September.[13] The three very different designs, extremely expensive to make, were highly anthropomorphic: each one suggested the person occupying the chair and their likely activities. But if the programme was Le Corbusier's, it was Perriand and Jeanneret who worked out the details, and Perriand who had the prototypes made by her favourite craftsman, the antique dealer Labadie. Perriand chose the colours – brown or blue lacquer or chrome for the metal and a wide range of coverings for the upholstery, from blue, green or brown satin to linen, parchment or brown calfskin. It was Perriand, too, who delivered the high quality and sense of chic that was required. It is notable that Perriand remembered Le Corbusier describing the three prototype chairs as *coquet* ('pretty'), a gendered word normally used for female fashion.[14] This was also the word used by Marcel Zahar in *La Revue de la femme*, in September 1929, who wrote of Perriand's apartment: 'the dining room lures one in with its *coquet* character' ('*La salle à manger séduit par son caractère de coquetterie*').[15] Perriand kept two notebooks of sketches and notes that demonstrate her engagement with the details of production.[16] But if Perriand's initial contribution to the work of the Le Corbusier atelier depended on her skills as a decorative designer, she quickly adapted to the architectural principles of the master.

above   Le Corbusier, Pierre Jeanneret, Charlotte Perriand, *Fauteuil dossier basculant*, intended for the Villa Church, 1928
below   Anonymous, Colonial chair. Reference model for the design of the *Fauteuil dossier basculant*

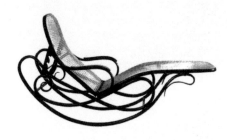

The first deployment of the three chairs, and a new table largely designed by Perriand, was in the music pavilion for Henry and Barbara Church. Perriand had already provided the guest pavilion at Villa Church with her leather-upholstered swivel chairs and a dining table, as well as cove lighting and built-in cupboards. The design of this table was improved for the music pavilion with a frame of oval-section tube supporting a thick cast-glass slab. This was cast flat and retained golden flecks of sand on the under-side. The room was given a slick, modern look with polished aluminium doors to the book-shelves. In this room, Le Corbusier finally faced up to the challenge of meeting his clients' expectations of modernity combined with luxury. This did not stop Henry Church complaining about the cost of the materials. Once again, the effect of Perriand's contribution was to make Le Corbusier's austere design more welcoming and to give it more impact.

We do not have the precise details of the arrangement between Perriand and Le Corbusier, but we do know that she had a unique position in the atelier. Le Corbusier began to separate the interior design from the rest and to charge his clients a five per cent fee for it. Perriand was given individual credit for this work and it is possible that she received all or part of the payments. On 16 May 1929, Le Corbusier wrote to Henry Church explaining why the interior design fees were so high:

> Our work includes both buildings and their furnishing. The truth is that the interior demands infinitely more care than the exterior; it requires more architectural quality and a considerable amount of time. [...] Your furniture belongs to models that we created with Ms Perriand. This project, which dates back to some years ago, requires changes and innovations each day.[17]

None of Le Corbusier's other draughtspeople at this time – among whom were significant architects, such as Josep Lluís Sert, Ernest Weissmann, Albert Frey and Alfred Roth – was given a similar status. In the 'black book' in which the draughtspeople's presentation drawings were logged, Perriand was referred to, young though she was, as 'Mme Perriand'. Her name is also included in the patent applications made for the furniture. This was not the case with other patent applications, such as that for horizontally sliding windows, on which several draughtspeople worked but only Le Corbusier and Jeanneret were credited.

In October 1929, this collaborative design process achieved its apotheosis in the model apartment exhibited at the Salon d'Automne. Le Corbusier probably had a hand in the overall plan of the apartment, but he left for a lecture tour in Argentina and Brazil before any of the detailed design had begun. In addition to the three chairs, Perriand's swivel chair and the glass table already installed in the Villa Church, Perriand developed an exquisite set of unit furniture, constructed of a chromed metal frame with glass shelves and a fully detailed kitchen and bedroom.[18] The bed ran on a rail so that it could be moved out to make it easier to make the bed. The floor of the living room

left   Le Corbusier, Pierre Jeanneret, Charlotte Perriand, first version of the *Chaise longue basculante*, 1928
right   Thonet rocking chair, c.1880

was lined with the same type of glass slabs as those used for the table. Taking a leaf from the book of Le Corbusier, who inserted personal objects – his glasses or a pipe – Perriand 'signed' the photographs of the apartment with her famous 'ball bearing' necklace, made out of chromed copper balls, and put one of her dresses in the bedroom cupboard. The success of the exhibit prompted the trustees of the Salon des artistes décorateurs, which had rejected the Le Corbusier team's project in March 1929, to invite Walter Gropius and his Bauhaus team to design a similar apartment in 1930.

Thonet-Mundus, which had met the costs of the Salon d'Automne exhibition, had acquired the right to manufacture and market the furniture. Perriand corresponded with them for several years, but very few pieces were sold. To some extent this was due to the effect of the Wall Street Crash, but it was also because Thonet's aim, in buying up the best tubular-steel designs in Europe, was in part to eliminate competition for their wooden furniture.

The Salon d'Automne exhibition was the high point and also the end of the 'furniture adventure'. It presents in an almost perfect form a conception of modern design that was at once functional and humanistic, machine-like but also evocative of the softness of the human body. Mary McLeod has demonstrated that the Salon d'Automne apartment made a decisive impact on the French and international press. It became a litmus test of modernity: conservative critics like Léandre Vaillat and Camille Mauclair condemned it as mechanical and inhumane, while others such as Max Terrier called it 'a manifesto ... a declaration of war on the ideal of the padded and stuffed bourgeois salon'.[19]

Le Corbusier, Pierre Jeanneret, Charlotte Perriand, first-floor library in the music pavilion of the Villa Church, 1928

But change was in the air. Le Corbusier was already beginning to rediscover the qualities of natural materials – brick, stone and wood – in his project for Maison Errazuriz (1930) and the house he designed for Hélène de Mandrot near Toulon (1929–31).[20] Perriand was shocked when she visited the old people's home in Frankfurt designed by Mart Stam and others, finding it inhumane and cold. She and Pierre Jeanneret were moving to the left politically and towards the vernacular aesthetically. Joan Ockman has brilliantly traced the relationships between political engagement and a search for the authenticity and warmth of natural materials and for the workmanship of vernacular architecture.[21] Perriand dreamed of moving to the Soviet Union, as many German architects did in 1929. But during her two trips to Moscow, in 1930 and 1934, she realised that communism, inspiring in theory, could not deliver in practice. This did not stop her from engaging actively in left-wing politics and, later, embracing the hope and high expectations of the Popular Front.[22]

We do not know exactly what Perriand's contribution was to the many architectural projects brought to fruition by the studio between 1929 and 1933. Jacques Barsac sees her hand in a large number of drawings, mostly concerning furniture, but she did collaborate also on architectural projects.[23] We know that Le Corbusier gave her a little pavilion to design for STAR, an air company at Le Bourget airport, and that he criticised her scheme and had Jeanneret do a slightly revised version.[24] She was also given a house-extension project for Julián Martinez, a close friend of Victoria Ocampo, who had welcomed Le Corbusier during his lecture tour in Buenos Aires.[25] The brief was to construct a living area and roof terrace over a garage, providing a garçonnière (bachelor pad) for Martinez and his mistress. There was to be no kitchen, but a small pool was planned for the roof terrace. The central part of the living room ceiling was lowered by 1.5 metres (5 feet) to accommodate the pool and two flower beds on the roof terrace. This left a low space for the bedroom 2.3 metres high (7.5 feet).

Windows from the flower beds on the roof terrace provided light. Perriand designed a room divider, consisting of the casiers developed for the Salon d'Automne apartment. She also put the bed on rollers, again as in the Salon d'Automne exhibit.

Perriand's finished drawings for the Martinez villa were logged in the studio 'black book' under her name.[26] Her name also appears in the 'black book' in reference to the Venesta exhibition stand (International Building Trade exhibition, Olympia, 1930) and to some drawings for Le Corbusier's apartment, the Salvation Army hospital, the Swiss Pavilion and one of the projects for Barcelona.[27] Perriand made a number of drawings for the interior of Le Corbusier's penthouse apartment, most of which were rejected by him, but did the detailing work in the kitchen. She worked extensively on the tubular-steel beds and other fittings in the Salvation Army Hostel, as well as planning work on the crèche and on an unexecuted project called the Cité Hospitalière that would have extended the hospital to the north. The research she carried out on the plight of unmarried mothers and orphans stimulated her move to the left politically. She almost certainly designed the kitchen for the weekend house for Albin Peyron, son of the general of the Salvation Army, in 1935. Barsac argues that she intervened in many other projects, including the Maisons Loucheur (1928–9) and the Ferme Radieuse (1934). The Le Corbusier atelier was a collective affair and there is no doubt that she had a marked influence on all the interior design schemes and furniture designs, whether or not she prepared the finished drawings.

It is also clear that Perriand took responsibility for exhibitions that presented the work of the atelier. At the first exhibition of the Union des artistes modernes (UAM), ten copies of the atelier's Fauteuil au dos basculant greeted the visitor at the entrance. Their stand consisted of Perriand's extendable dining table, her swivel chairs and a chaise longue. In 1931, Perriand worked on a small stand at the Internationale Raumausstellung in

Cologne, where she presented the *Fauteuil au dos basculant* and the *Chaise longue*, as well as two of the *casier* unit elements mounted on chrome legs.[28] In 1935, with Le Corbusier again absent, she and Jeanneret designed a stand entitled *Maison de jeune homme* (House for a young man) for the Exposition Universelle at Brussels.[29] The tone was now explicitly didactic: a large blackboard on the wall explained the plan as a possible standard type. Even the table was made of slate, so that the occupants could express themselves. Although she included one of her tubular-steel swivelling chairs, the other pieces were bought off the shelf: a wooden armchair and unit cupboards made by the company Flambo. On the wall was a celebration of nature consisting of a painting by Fernand Léger and some rocks and bones. In this exhibit, Perriand used the mushroom-shaped 'Corolle' support employed for the marble dining tables in Le Corbusier's apartment, the meeting room of the Swiss Pavilion and the weekend house for Mr Felix in La Celle Saint-Cloud.

Perriand worked extensively on one project, no doubt motivated in part by her political ideals. This was the set of apartment plans based on a minimum area of 14 square metres (150 square feet) per person.[30] A driving force behind modern architecture was the commitment to solve the housing question. Le Corbusier had devoted a lot of attention to the problem

and, by 1930, he had designed a system of long blocks of flats in a parkland setting that he called 'The Radiant City'. But he had not developed the interior design in any detail. Perriand devoted more than 100 sheets of sketches to the problem of creating a set of modular apartments for varying sizes of family, from single people to families of seven or eight children. The module allocated fourteen square metres per person. Perriand was motivated by her political views to provide genuinely affordable housing units within Le Corbusier's housing blocks. Most of these drawings remained in her possession, and it is not clear how far this work was supported by Le Corbusier.[31] He discussed the project, however, in two articles in the magazine *Plans*.[32] When he republished these articles in his book *La Ville Radieuse* (The Radiant City, 1935), he acknowledged Perriand's collaboration.

Perriand was allowed to undertake some private commissions. She designed some built-in cupboards for the Martel brothers, an office for the editor of *La Semaine de Paris* and an apartment for the composer Jean Rivier, among others. In these projects, she used her swivel chair and developed the metal unit furniture, often with striking coloured or metallic doors.

Perriand's growing scepticism about the inhumanity of some modern architecture went hand in hand with a rediscovery of

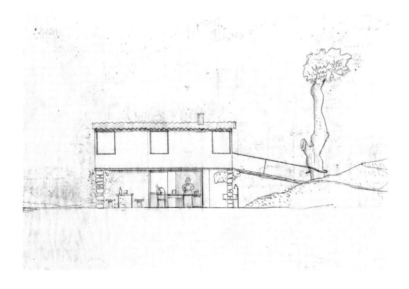

Cross-section of the *Maison au bord de l'eau* (House by the water), 1934

vernacular buildings. With Jeanneret, she drew and photographed traditional houses in the valleys of the Jura and Haute-Savoie. They also followed Le Corbusier and their friend Fernand Léger in studying, collecting and photographing natural forms – rocks, shells and driftwood.[33] This experience influenced several architectural projects they undertook together. Perriand designed a number of weekend cottages in prefabricated materials, sometimes in collaboration with Jeanneret. In 1935, she was awarded the silver prize in a competition for a weekend house. Her ingenious scheme for *Maison au bord de l'eau* (House by the water) had two lightweight structures housing a kitchen-dining room and six beds flanking an open area.[34] This space could be protected from the sun by large folding panels that also served to close the house up in the winter months. She designed

various versions of this project and even tried to manufacture it in the 1960s. A version of *Maison au bord de l'eau* was constructed in 2013; it was exhibited in Miami and at the recent exhibition at the Fondation Louis Vuitton in Paris. Following the legislation passed by the Popular Front to offer all workers paid leave, she worked up a project for a vacation centre using rough stone walls and prefabricated wooden panels.[35] On a similar theme, she worked on a number of Alpine refuges (1936–7).[36] Some of these were of simple wooden construction, but two were made of prefabricated insulated aluminium panels on a tubular framework of Duralumin. The panels had to be small and light enough to be transported to altitude in the Alps by mule. André Tournon, an expert in aluminium construction, worked with her on this. A prototype of the Refuge Bivouac was

Study room in the *Maison du jeune homme* (House for a young man), 1935.
The revolving display, anchored to the floor and ceiling, presents a photomontage on the history of the development of human societies, methods of production and means of communication

assembled on the banks of the Seine during the 1937 exhibition and a modified version assembled near Perriand's Alpine chalet at Saint-Nicolas de Véroce in the Haute-Savoie. In 1938, she and Jeanneret designed a more elaborate mountain refuge.[37] Circular in plan, it was mounted on a central column and braced with tension wires. Big enough to accommodate twenty to thirty people in bunks deployed on two levels, it was extremely lightweight. The exterior consisted of aluminium panels insulated with glass wool and Isorel board or pine planks. She continued to work on projects associated with sport, the Alps and leisure until the war.

Perriand engaged actively in the didactic effort to persuade working people to improve their homes. In 1936, she launched a questionnaire and published the results on 22 May. She published an article in the communist journal *Vendredi*, '*l'organe des hommes libres s'adressant à des hommes libres*' ('the voice of free men talking to free men'), illustrating a set of practical suggestions for improving conditions in home interiors. Specifically addressing women, she presented plans of the *casiers* she had designed with Le Corbusier and suggested that people could have them built by local carpenters or even make them themselves. She backed this up with an appeal

for better standards of hygiene, lighting and ventilation in housing. With the election of the Popular Front, social consciousness was gaining ground and obtaining some support.

Perriand followed this up with a stand at the very popular Salon des arts ménagers.[38] This was a three metre by four metre (ten by thirteen foot) apartment for 'people of modest means'. Again selecting standard Flambo metal storage units, she used colour to add gaiety and variety. A wooden dining table, the same as the one for Ange and Paul Gutmann, contrasted with one of the standard tubular-steel tables. The very simple folding tubular-steel chair, based on a modest deckchair, had been designed in 1928 but never manufactured until now. At the same exhibition, she launched herself into a giant photomural – *La misère de Paris* – with the support of like-minded young architects some of whom, like Jean Bossu, worked in Le Corbusier's atelier.[39] Combining photographs, diagrams, slogans and texts, she presented a devastating critique of the City of Lights, its pollution, slum housing and disease. She also obtained the patronage of the new minister of agriculture, Georges Monnet, and designed photocollage murals for the vestibule of his office. On these, giant photographs are interspersed with graphs and texts promoting Monnet's new law fixing

left   Kitchen area opening on to the living room in Le Vieux Matelot, Saint-Nicolas-de-Véroce, 1938
right   Le Vieux Matelot, Saint-Nicolas-de-Véroce, 1938. Suspended dovecote for mountain dwellers in love

3

agricultural prices. It was Monnet who enabled Perriand to obtain a site, at the last minute, for Le Corbusier's Pavillon des Temps Nouveaux (Pavilion of the New Times), at the Universal Exhibition in Paris in 1937. It was, in fact, Perriand who was nominated chief architect of the pavilion. Le Corbusier had become increasingly upset about the political turn taken by some of his assistants, whom he saw as forming a group in opposition to him. He wrote a long letter to Perriand and Jeanneret expressing this view, and Perriand immediately resigned.

In the last two years before the war, Perriand continued to work on prefabricated light-weight structures. One of her most beautiful works, however, was the little house she built for herself and her friends at Saint-Nicolas de Véroce.[40] A simple structure of stone walls framed a living-dining-cooking area on the ground floor and three bedrooms on the first floor. On the south side, a four-metre (thirteen-foot) door composed of alternating glazed and coloured rectangles was designed to swing open on to a terrace, boarded to provide a windscreen. Closed, it framed the scenery in spectacular fashion. Perriand designed

a magnificent free-form dining table, initiating one of the leitmotifs of her work in Japan during the war and after.

Charlotte Perriand's great contributions to the development of modern architecture and design came in part from her attention to detail, materials and means of construction, but above all from her understanding of people's needs and desires. Her work invariably adds joy and satisfaction to buildings and objects that are intended to serve a useful purpose. Her collaboration with Le Corbusier and Pierre Jeanneret produced some of the most memorable and long-lasting pieces of furniture of the twentieth century. She helped make the 'classic' modernist works of Le Corbusier and Jeanneret – Villa Savoye, Villa Church, the Swiss Pavilion and the 1929 Salon d'Automne apartment – more humane and significantly more welcoming. Her social engagement contributed greatly to the equipment of the Salvation Army Hostel and to the exhibitions of the short-lived Popular Front. She had the flexibility to adapt to new conditions during the 1930s and to work with different materials. By 1939, she was ready to branch out more completely on her own.

Abbreviations
AChP: Archives Charlotte Perriand, Paris
FLC: Fondation Le Corbusier, Paris

1 For an introduction to Perriand's work, see Mary McLeod (ed.), *Charlotte Perriand: An Art of Living* (New York: Harry N. Abrams, 2003).

2 Ibid., 10.

3 Charlotte Perriand, *A Life of Creation* (New York: Monacelli Press, 2003).

4 Two of Loos's most influential articles were published in Paris in the early 1920s: 'Ornament and Crime' (a lecture of 1908) and 'Architecture' (1910).

5 Charlotte Perriand, 'Wood or Metal?', *The Studio*, 97 (1929), 278–9.

6 For Perriand's work from 1926 to 1929, see Jacques Barsac, *Charlotte Perriand: Complete Works, Volume 1, 1903–1940* (Zurich: Scheidegger & Spiess, 2014), 36–50.

7 Patent in Perriand's married name of Scholefield, 29 May 1928 (AChP), see Arthur Rüegg, *Charlotte Perriand: Livre de Bord*, 1928–1933 (Basel: Birkhäuser, 2004), 25.

8 FLC 33499, reproduced in Le Corbusier, *Precisions: On the Present State of Architecture and City Planning* (Zurich: Park Books, 2015),119 [original French edition: 1930].

9 Arthur Rüegg, 'Un équipement intérieur d'une habitation: new furniture for a new world', in *Charlotte Perriand: Inventing a New World*, ed. Jacques Barsac, Sébastien Cherruet and Pernette Perriand (Paris: Foundation Louis Vuitton and Gallimard, 2019), 53–64.

10 For a detailed analysis of these chairs, see Mary McLeod, 'New designs for living', in McLeod (2003), 36–63, and Rüegg (2004), 24–40.

11 Published in Le Corbusier et al., *Oeuvre complète* (Zurich: Éditions Girsberger, 1930), 207. A version of this sketch was used in his lecture tour of South America in October–November 1929 (FLC 33498).

12 Photo AChP. A patent application in the name of the three architects was submitted on 28 February 1929 (AChP 28 013). See Barsac (2014), 77.

13 AChP 28 025.

14 Charlotte Perriand, *Une Vie de création* (Paris: Odile Jacob, 1998), 33. A strand of cultural studies has worked on the gender constructions of modernism, offsetting the 'masculine' modes of modernist rationalism against the 'feminine' construction of the decorative arts. See, among others, Deborah Fausch et al., *Architecture in Fashion* (Princeton, NJ: Princeton University Press, 1994); Mark Wigley, *White Walls, Designer Dresses* (Cambridge, MA: MIT Press, 1995); Brenda Martin and Penny Sparke (eds), *Women's Places: Architecture and Design 1860–1960* (London: Routledge, 2003).

15 Marcel Zahar, *La Revue de la femme*, 31 (September 1929), 31 and 50, cited in ibid.

16 These notebooks are reproduced and commented on in Rüegg (2004).

17 FLC H3/03/70. 'Nos travaux comprennent tant les bâtiments que leur aménagement intérieur. Ce qui est vrai, c'est que l'intérieur exige infiniment plus de soins que l'extérieur, exige plus de qualité d'architecte et demande un temps considérable. [...] Vos meubles appartiennent à des modèles que nous avons crée avec Mme Perriand. Cette création remonte à des années, et nécessite chaque jour des modifications ou des innovations'

18 Rüegg (2004), 49–53, and Barsac (2014), 74–109.

19 McLeod (2003), 62.

20 Tim Benton, 'The Villa de Mandrot and the Place of the Imagination', in *Massilia*, ed. Michel Richard (Marseille: Éditions Imbernon, 2011), 92–105.

21 Joan Ockman, 'Lessons from Objects: Perriand from the Pioneer Years to the "Epoch of Realities"', in McLeod (2003), 154–81.

22 Danilo Udovicki-Selb, '"C'était dans l'air": Charlotte Perriand and the Popular Front', in McLeod (2003), 68–89.

23 Barsac (2014), 178–233.

24 Société de transports aériens rapides, in Barsac (2014), 178–81.

25 Barsac (2014), 182–9.

26 See *Studio*, 2397–2400 (May 1930) and 2510–2516 (October 1930).

27 Barsac (2014), 118–234.

28 Ibid., 192–3.

29 Ibid., 342–7.

30 Ibid., 126–33, and Sébastien Gokalp, 'The True Measure: The 14-Square-Meter Cellule per Inhabitant', in Barsac, Cherruet and Perriand (2019), 81–7.

31 A few of her sketches are retained in the archives of the Fondation Le Corbusier (e.g. FLC 28225–6 and 28231).

32 Le Corbusier, 'Vivre', *Plans*, 4 (April 1931), and Le Corbusier, 'L'élément biologique: la cellule de 14m² par habitant', *Plans*, 9 (November 1931).

33 Jacques Barsac, *Charlotte Perriand et la photographie: l'oeil en eventail* (Milan: 5 continents, 2011), and Tim Benton, *LC foto: Le Corbusier: secret photographer* (Baden: Lars Müller, 2013).

34 Barsac (2014), 302–7.

35 Ibid., 308–11.

36 Ibid., 316–25.

37 Ibid., 332–7.

38 Ibid., 354–7.

39 For Perriand's engagement with large-scale photo-murals, see Barsac, Cherruet and Perriand (2019), 213–42.

40 Barsac (2014), 438–47.

notebooks 1930–1940

jacques barsac

Many artists and designers keep notebooks in order to jot down ideas, emotions and discoveries that feed into the creative process. For the historian, these notebooks can sometimes help to reconstitute the genesis of a project, allowing us to retrace its sources and follow its subsequent evolution.

Until 1944, Charlotte Perriand kept illustrated notebooks (some more illustrated than others) that punctuated the key moments in her life: trips to Moscow, Greece, Japan and Indochina. In her youth, she drew everything that crossed her path, filling her notebooks with sketches of animals, people and landscapes, encouraged by her teachers at the Union centrale des arts décoratifs. During her time at the Académie de la Grande Chaumière, she learnt to draw nudes in the space of a minute, a way of developing her eye, going straight to the essential and capturing the decisive character-istics of a subject. But drawing alone was not enough. In the interwar years, photography became a sort of logbook that allowed her to memorise her enchantments, her discoveries and her Alpine exploits.[1] Pragmatic, with no time to waste, she used her 6 × 6 camera to capture the sculptural force of a bridge structure, the poetry of a tree canopy, the curve of a sail in the wind, the geometric lines of fishing nets stretched out on the beach, the functional elegance of the skeleton of a fish or the rational efficiency of a chicken's wishbone, living mechanics that were useful to understand when building a chair.

'I keep a vigilant eye on everything,' wrote Perriand in Japan in 1941. 'One does not invent, one discovers, and the discoveries are multiple. I also keep myself in a state of creation outside of formulae, a creation that is constantly renewed by the fecund shocks of life.'[2] She used the deft expression *avoir l'œil en éventail* – literally 'to keep the eye deployed like a fan' – to describe an important aspect of her creative process. *L'œil en éventail*, as recorded in her notebooks and photographs, involved looking closely at every object, from the most humble to the most remarkable, from the smallest to the largest, those

fashioned by nature and those made by human hand, so as to discover the hidden virtues that could be reproduced in other objects whose function was often very different – such as her Refuge Tonneau of 1938, which was inspired by a children's carousel photographed on a Croatian beach the year before.

From 1928 to 1930, she kept two 'logbooks' during the design process for the famous tubular-steel furniture created while she was working with Le Corbusier and Pierre Jeanneret. The first, which numbers seventy pages, concerns the chairs and tables, and begins with cut-out images of existing furniture that are annotated with the price and the name of the company.[3] The first model included is Thonet's famous bentwood B9 Chair, which Le Corbusier and Perriand particularly appreciated and which Le Corbusier and Jeanneret had used in many of their archi-tectural projects. Further into the notebook we find the advertising prospectus *Meubles en métal Thonet* (Thonet metal furniture), which includes new chairs and tables in curved, nickelled steel by Mart Stam and the Bauhaus's Marcel Breuer, along with their prices. Likewise, Perriand mentions the prices and techniques for recent metal furniture by Pierre Chareau, identifying the competition that her future creations would have to contend with on the market.

Making furniture using cold-bent steel was a new technique that sought to replace traditional woodworking methods. Given designers' and metalworkers' consequent lack of experience in the field, Perriand carefully noted down all the attempts that had been made to perfect designs and simplify manufacture. The pages of her notebook, which are abundantly illustrated with annotated sketches, list all the various attempts, the results and the modifications she deemed necessary. Her notes are punctu-ated with critical judgements: 'Impractical', 'The buckle tears', 'Try with Duco or chromed springs', 'make disassembly possible so as to facilitate chroming and polishing'. Unlike

Breuer and Stam, who used screws to join their steel tubes, Perriand opted to weld hers, a choice that widened the aesthetic possibilities but also considerably increased the cost of manufacture, since sanding down the welds was very labour-intensive. Today her metal furniture – the pivoting chaise longue, the *Grand confort* armchair, the aeroplane-tube table, the armchair with the pivoting back – is known the world over, but its lack of commercial success at the time meant that she did not pursue the promising leads sketched out in her notebook.

The sixty-page logbook for the design of the metal storage units begins with a sheet of female silhouettes captioned with brief commentaries such as: 'a 1.65-metre tall standing woman takes [an object] at 1.80 metres [reaching upwards with her arm], [and] at 0.55 metre [when leaning forward]', 'A 1.65-metre tall standing woman sees [her environment] at [a height of] 1.35 metres [and] at 0.55 metre [below]'. At this point in her career, most of Perriand's design sketches for domestic interiors begin with male and female silhouettes with an eye drawn in, and are configured with respect to these factors. The logbook pages immediately following the silhouettes consist of an inventory of everyday objects that would need to be stored in the metal units – books, clothing, kitchen utensils, plates, bottles – along with their dimensions. As in the logbook for the chairs and tables, the listing of these characteristics is an essential part of the brief, which sets out the furniture's design parameters. The two types of preliminary study in the storage-unit logbook demonstrate the key importance of the characteristics of the human body in the way she calculated the dimensions of the units – a highly rational approach based on the intersection of the morphological specifications of bodies and objects. Perriand summarised her research method in the slogan 'Gesture, form, technique', the factoring in of these three variables, along with cost, leading to the object's design.[4] Her sketches and handwriting reveal the freshness of the instant, the excitement of discovery, that magic moment when ideas crystallise,

while the telegraphic style of her comments often betrays a certain urgency and tension.

Perriand's first Japan notebook begins in Tokyo on 5 September 1940, a few days after her arrival, and ends on 21 October of that same year, at the conclusion of her first trip to the archipelago. There would follow other notebooks that described her activities during her stay. The first begins by retracing the work she undertook for her consultancy mission on the reform of Japanese craftsmanship and education with respect to the production of objects and furnishings for the home. Several pages describe the shock of visiting the Mingeikan, the Japan Folk Crafts Museum, where she met its founder, Sōetsu Yanagi. It was an ideal place to discover the history of Japanese folk craft in particular and Asian folk craft in general, and in her notes Perriand describes her fascination with craftsmanship and vernacular expression, and attempts to theorise the reasons behind the forms and beauty of the pieces she saw.

Until Perriand arrives in Kyoto, on Wednesday, 25 September 1940, her notebook appears blind to the image in preference to the word: there is not a single drawing. Suddenly, a visit to the Katsura Imperial Villa produces a plethora of sketches. She notes: 'Visit to the imperial palace, Katsura Imperial Villa. A beautiful example of architecture. Here the moderns can easily continue the tradition. We recognise our precepts.'[5] The relationship between text and drawing was now reversed: in rapid sketches she jotted down the characteristics that struck her and listed the similarities to modern architecture. Ideas poured forth on to the notebook's pages, such as the table with an interchangeable top, the bamboo bed, the folding chairs and the bamboo lamp that she would have made for her exhibition, since the Takashimaya department store had just accepted her proposal to organise a show illustrating her ideas for the reform of Japanese production.[6]

On 2 October 1940, she sketched Katsura's *tokonoma* – the alcove in which revered objects were displayed – about which she said, 'the boards perform like clouds. The diagonal piece of furniture divides the space.' Over a decade later, it would inspire her famous *Nuage* (cloud) bookshelves, which reproduced the misalignment of the wooden shelves – a hymn to asymmetry – and linked them with supports in folded sheet-metal.

Following her astonishment at discovering Japanese craftsmanship, she noted down a conversation with the French ambassador in Tokyo, who displayed all the disdain of the elite towards common people. For him, folklore did not represent Japanese art, and there could be no art without an author, without real artists. To which Perriand rejoined, 'In my opinion, Art is in everything. Making love well is an Art ... Cooking well is an Art ... Living well is an Art ...'.

Her notebooks are peppered with remarks that go far beyond the epigrammatic and express her view of the world. The first Japanese notebook ends with a reference to the political situation, omitting too much detail due to censorship: 'Spoke to [Sōri] Yanagi about young people in Japan. Serious problem. For the young leaving art school, the only options are employment in munitions factories and five years' military service.' Fourteen months later, the Japanese attack on Pearl Harbor would mark the beginning of the Pacific War.

1   See Jacques Barsac, *Charlotte Perriand et la photographie: l'œil en éventail* (Milan: 5 Continents, 2011).
2   *Contact avec l'Art japonais: Sélection, Tradition, Création* (Tokyo: Éditions Kujio Koyama, 1941), commentaire planche 21.
3   Arthur Rüegg, *Charlotte Perriand: livre de bord, 1928–1933* (Paris: Éditions Infolio, 2004).
4   Charlotte Perriand, 'L'art d'habiter', *Technique et Architecture*, 9–10 (August 1950), 79.
5   Charlotte Perriand's notebooks, 1 October 1940.
6   The proposal was accepted on Saturday, 21 September 1940.

75 cm

B 9
(48 cm)

B 28
(41 cm)

N⁰ 88
Drucker 180 Rue des Pyrenées

330 Frs.

N⁰ 816.
Drucker

127 Frs.

Allez. Frères
1 Rue St Martin

35. Frs.

Perriand kept two portfolios of the furniture she developed while working for Le Corbusier. This one relates to tables and chairs, while another logs her cabinets. Running to seventy-two pages, it reveals her development process, starting with photographs from advertisements of chairs that were already on the market. Her sketches and notes show her attempts to perfect her tubular-metal designs, including comments such as 'Not practical'.

9

Ally-Frères

1 Rue St Martin

Toile dock. renforcé 38 et 78 Fr.

Ally. Frères.

95 Fr.

4

Sièges

Sièges pliants — de place possible —
confortables.

(A) ou paillasse...
installée comme dans les lits.

pivot

Avec ressosts siège et dossier

aut peut-être sans pivot.

On pourrait laisser le siège sans coussin en mettant.

$(2^{mm} 1/2.$

soit des sangles avec ressosts.

Ou tissu sangle —

avec oeillets à chaque extrémité

TABLES.

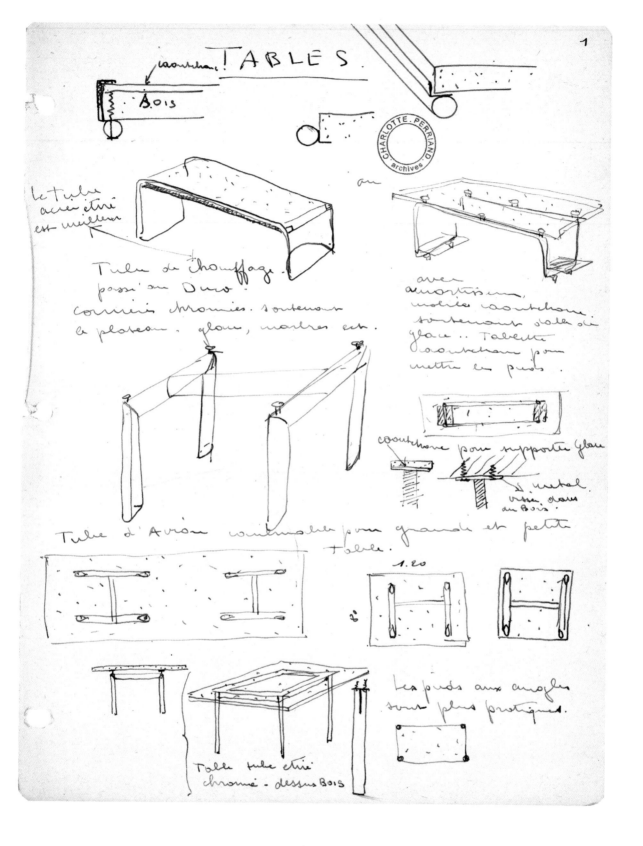

caoutchouc

BOIS

CHARLOTTE.PERRIAND. archives

Le tube
acier étiré
est meilleur

au

Tube de chauffage.
passé au Duco.
courriers chromées. soutenant
le plateau. glace, marbres etc.

avec
amortisseur,
molles caoutchouc
soutenant dalle de
glace.. Tablette
caoutchouc pour
mettre les pieds.

caoutchouc pour supporter glace

S. métal.
vissé dans
un Bois.

Tube d'Avion interminable pour grande et petite
table.

1.20

Les pieds aux angles
sont plus pratiques.

Table tube étiré
chromé - dessus Bois

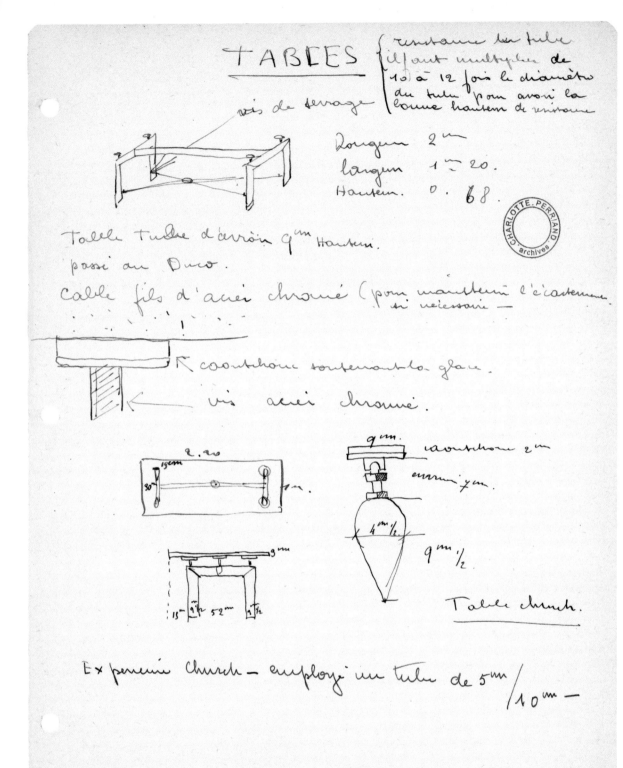

TABLES

(rentrant les tube
il faut multiplier de
10 à 12 fois le diamètre
du tube pour avoir la
bonne hauteur de rentrante

vis de serrage

Longueur 2ᵐ
largeur 1ᵐ.20.
Hauteur. 0.68.

Table Tube d'avion 9ᵐᵐ Hauteur.

passé au Duco.

Cable fils d'acier chromé (pour maintenir l'écartement
si nécessaire —

← caoutchouc soutenant la glace.

← vis acier chromé.

2.20

19ᶜᵐ

80ᵐ

1ᵐ

9ᵐᵐ caoutchouc 2ᵐᵐ
enroni 9ᵐ.

4ᵐᵐ.½

9ᵐᵐ ½

3ᵐᵐ

15ᵐᵐ 9½ 52ᵐᵐ 1½

Table chinch.

Experience Chinch — employé un tube de 5ᵐᵐ/10ᵐᵐ —

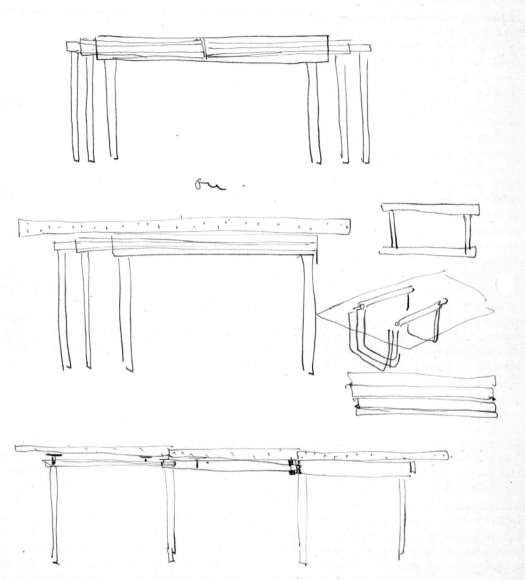

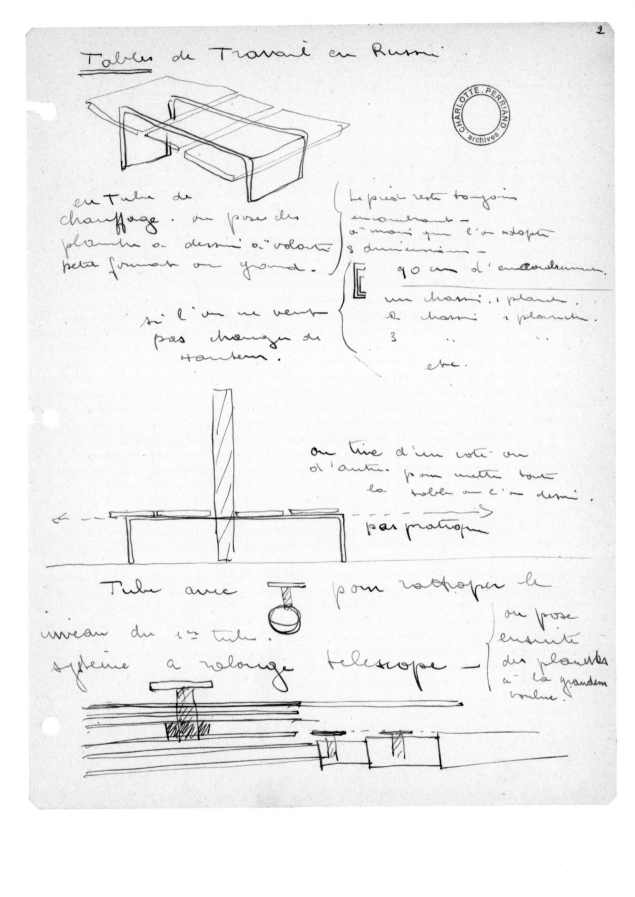

Tables de Travail en Russie.

en Tube de
chauffage. on pose des
planches à dessin à volonté
petit format ou grand.

si l'on ne veut
pas changer de
Hauteur.

Le pied reste toujours
encombrant —
à moins que l'on adopte
3 dimensions —

90 cm d'encombrement.

un chassis. 1 planche.
2 chassis 1 planche.
3   ..   ..
etc.

on tire d'un coté ou
d'autre. pour mettre toute
la table ou à ½ dessin.
par pratique

Tube avec   pour rattraper le
niveau du 1er tube.
système a rallonge telescope —

on pose
ensuite
des planches
à la grandeur
voulue.

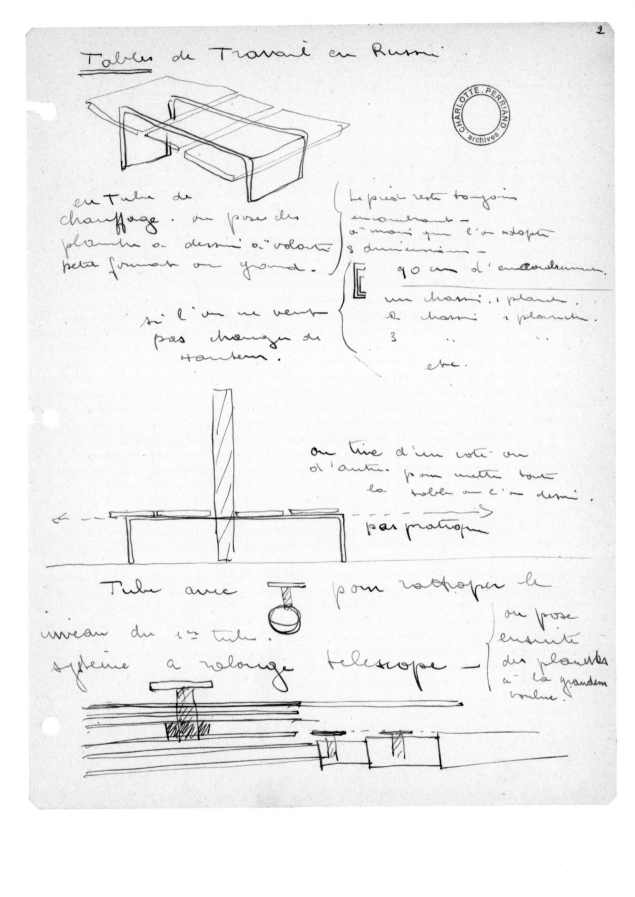

Table extensible

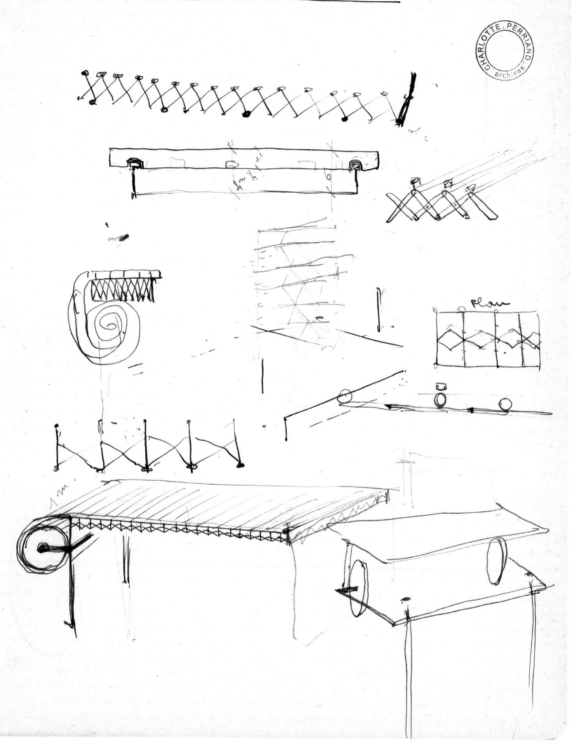

Plan

Laqué Blanc –
(Maison Blanc
PRIX. 155 FRS –

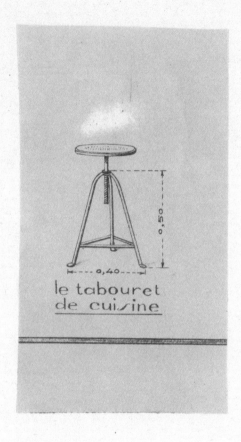

le tabouret
de cuisine

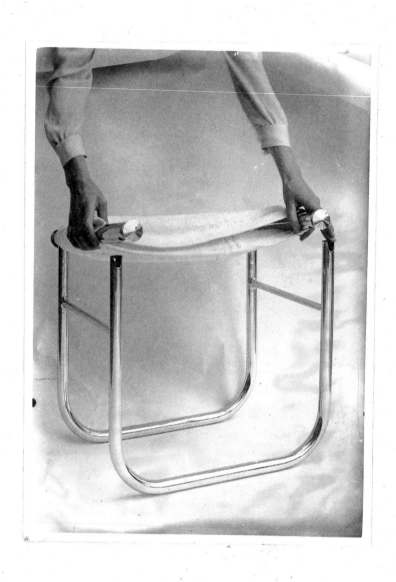

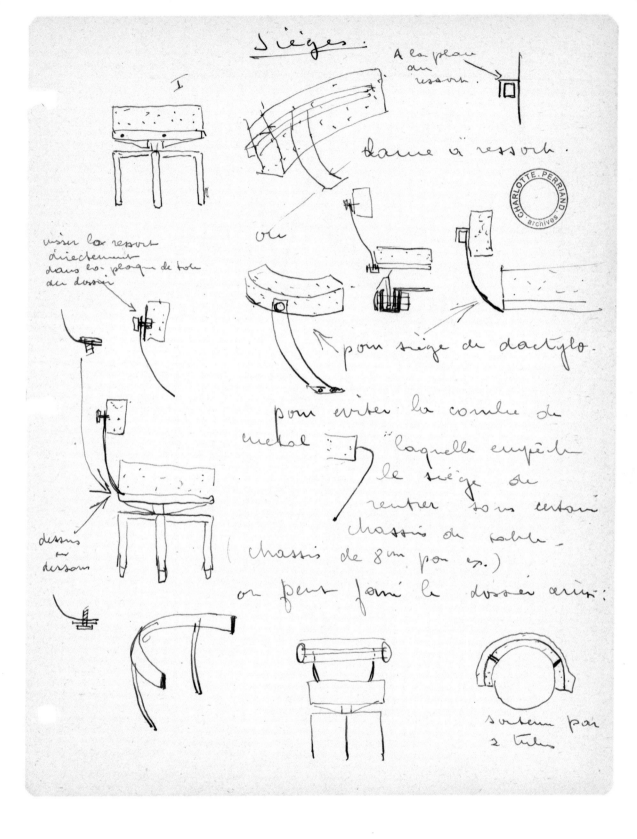

Sièges.

A la place du ressort.

lame à ressort.

visser le ressort directement dans la plaque de tôle du dossier

ou

pour siège de dactylo.

dessus ou dessous

pour éviter la courbe de métal "laquelle empêche le siège de rentrer sous certain chassis de table. (chassis de 8m par ex.) on peut faire le dossier ainsi:

soutenu par 2 tubes

Le Siège Dufaux

PARTIE MÉTALLIQUE DU SIÈGE DUFAUX

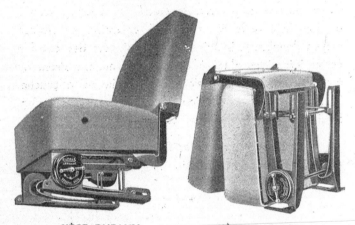

SIÈGE DUFAUX
garni

SIÈGE DUFAUX
rabattu et levé pour laisser le passage

———

Nous livrons la carcasse métallique des sièges DUFAUX aux carrossiers, constructeurs, selliers, garagistes, susceptibles de faire garnissage et tapisserie de ces sièges.

Sur demande, nous pouvons livrer les sièges complets avec carcasse de coussins.

Le Siège DUFAUX garni est à peine plus haut qu'un siège ordinaire.

Sièges

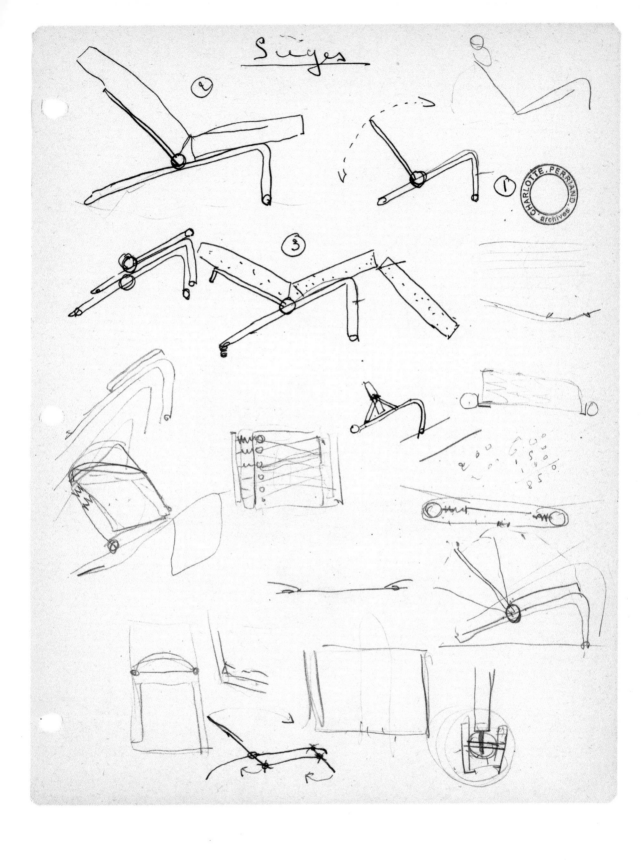

D.

Sièges

Bras fauteuil B —

la boucle arrivée — →

les 2 cercles employés comme les
boucles de ceinture ne donne pas
beaucoup de prise, surtout si le
tissu est rigide — ~~...~~

A essayer les ressorts — au Duco ou
chromé —

et faire dans certains cas la partie
où l'on pose la main (en cuir)
adopter pour le fauteuil B — les sangles
~~et~~ ressorts —

les faire démontables pour peut-être le
chromage et polissage —

faire en sangle et veaux mort-né
ou { sangle et paille de blé

en ~~sangle~~ seulement —
en coussin drap
en coussin satin
en coussin peau de tambour (parchemin)

matière

Sièges

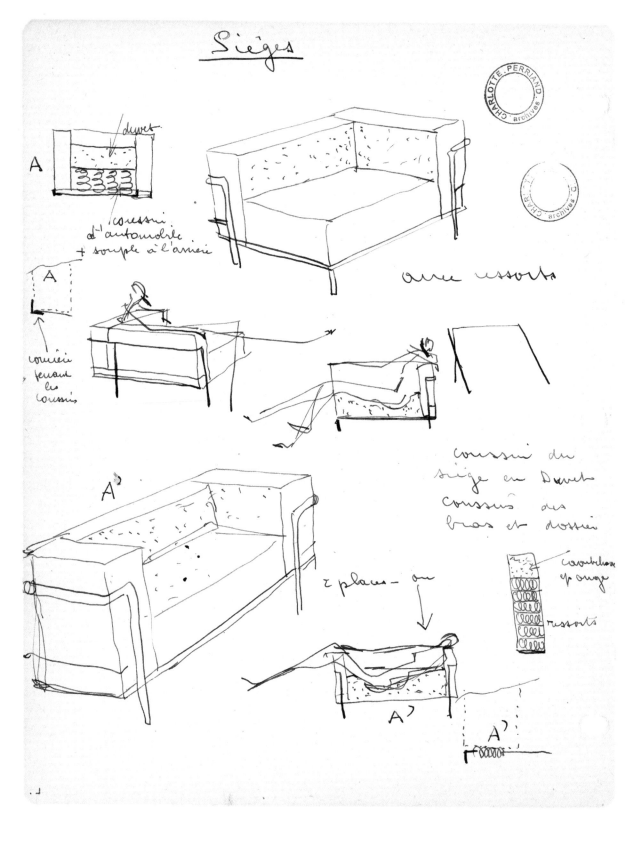

A

duvet

coussin d'automobile
+ souple à l'arrière

A

coussier fermant les coussins

avec ressorts

coussin du siège en Duvet
coussins des bras et dossier

A²

2 places – ou

A²

A²

Caoutchouc éponge

ressorts

L .

Sièges.

Chaise longue.

55

80

86

43

48

32

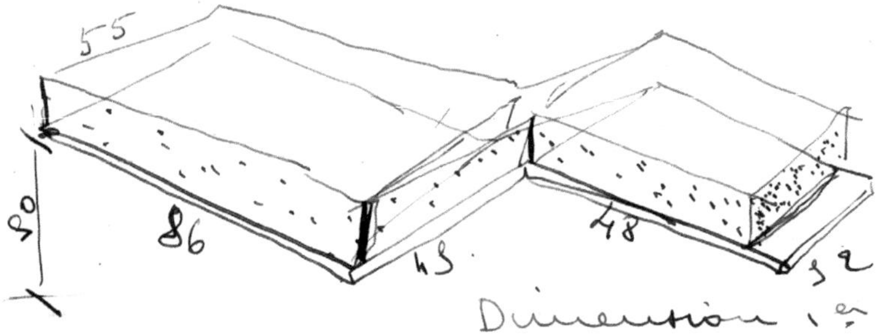

Dimension : 1er modèle —

chaise longue avec amortissem —

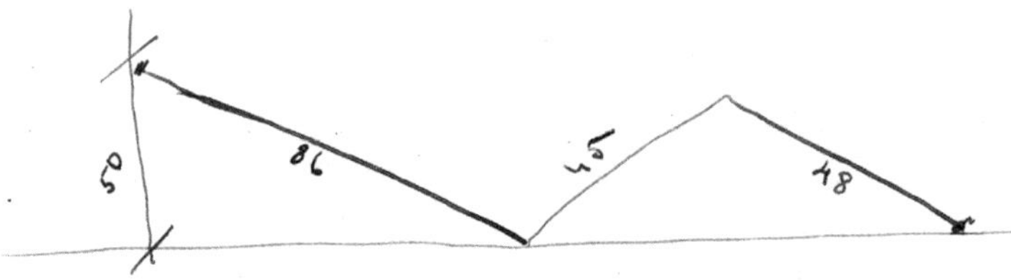

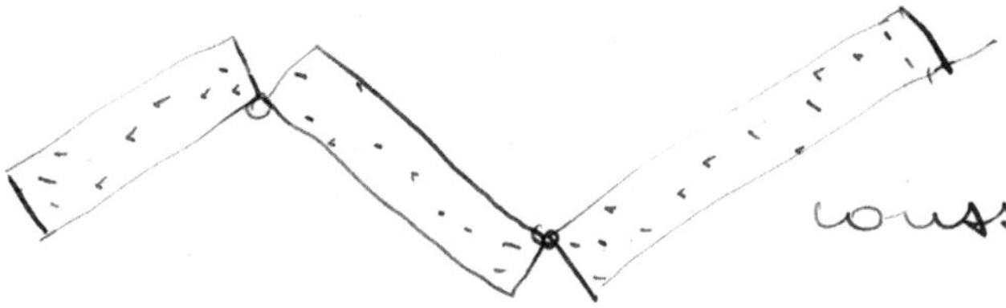

80

86

45

48

coussins articulé :

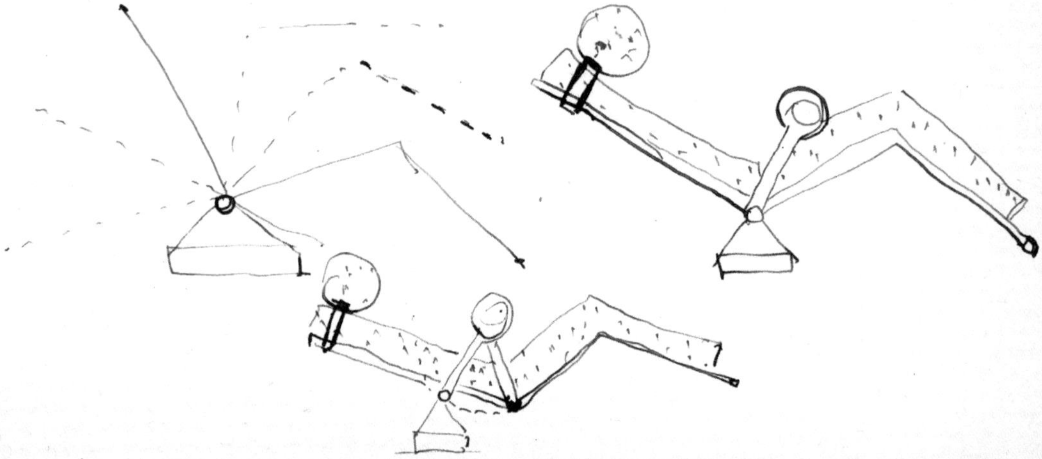

Sièges.

la chaise longue.

le centre de gravité
est légèrement déporté.

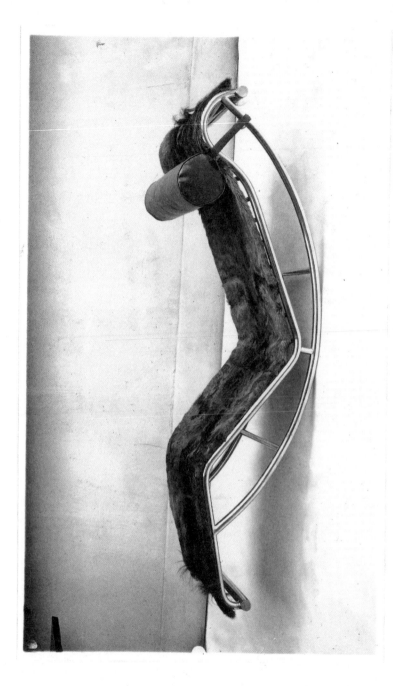

Sièges

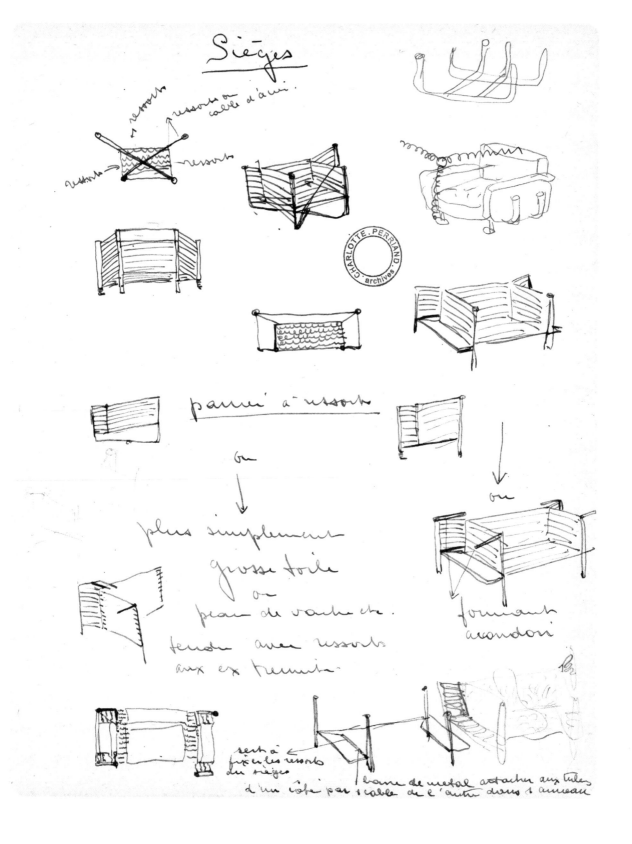

ressort

ressort ou
cable d'aci.

ressort

ressorts

panier à ressorts

ou

plus simplement
grosse toile
ou
peau de vache.
tendu avec ressorts
aux extremités

ou

formant
accordion

rest à
tendre les ressorts
du siège
d'un côté par cable de l'autre dans s anneau
barre de metal attaché aux tubes

CHARLOTTE·PERRIAND
archives

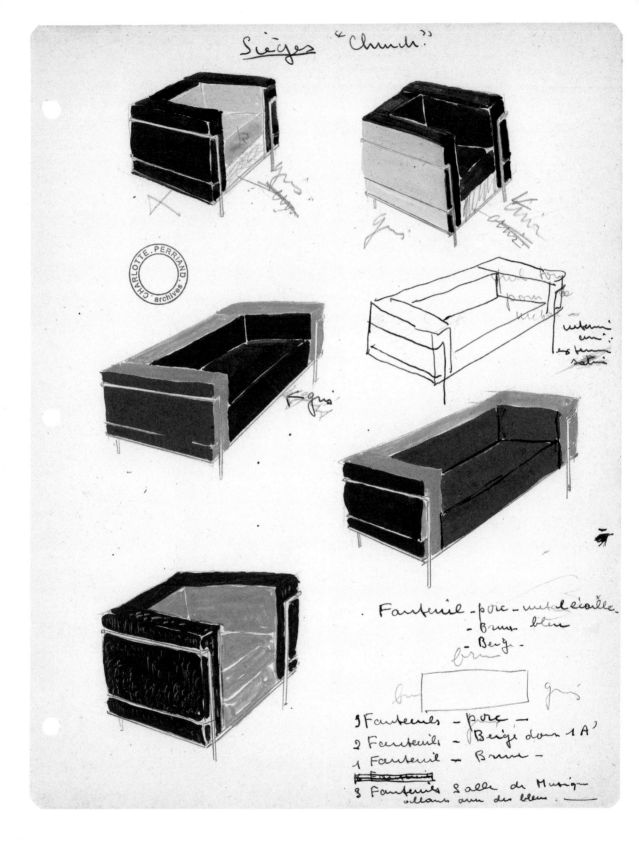

Sièges "Church"

Fauteuil - porc - metal écaillé
- Brun bleu
- Beige -

1 Fauteuils - porc -
2 Fauteuils - Beige dont 1 A'
1 Fauteuil - Brun -
3 Fauteuils Salle de Musique
allant avec des bleu.

Sièges Disponibles.

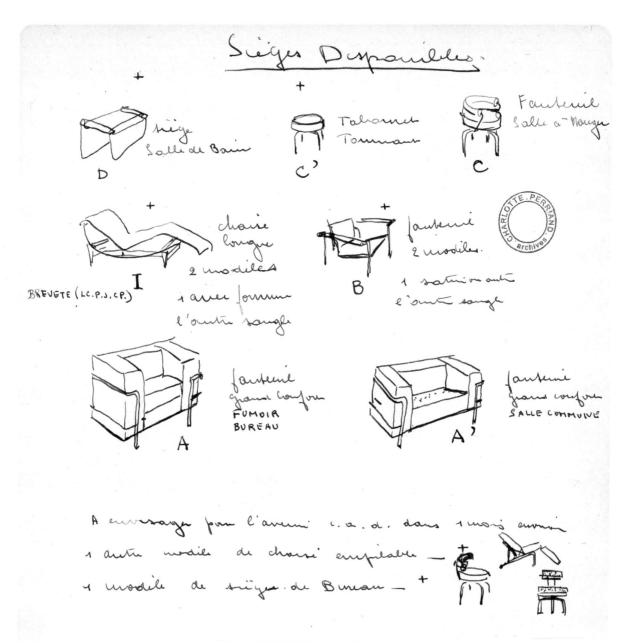

+   +

siège Salle de Bain — **D**

Tabouret Tournant — **C'**

Fauteuil Salle à Manger — **C**

chaise longue 2 modèles
1 avec fourrure
l'autre sangle

BREVETE (LC.P.J.CP.) **I**

fauteuil 2 modèles.
1 satin ou cuir
l'autre sangle — **B**

fauteuil grand confort
FUMOIR BUREAU — **A**

fauteuil grand confort
SALLE COMMUNE — **A'**

A envisager pour l'avenir c.a.d. dans 1 mois environ
1 autre modèle de chaise empilable —
1 modèle de sièges de Bureau — +

En acier Chromé —
" en Duco —

"Vi-Spring"

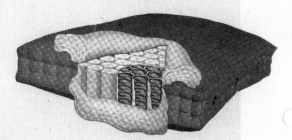

"Vi-Spring" Cushions can be made to practically any degree of softness or firmness desired, either for a base or top cushion. As a top cushion for Chairs, Chesterfields, etc., they are superior to Down Cushions, being nearly as soft and having the advantage of retaining their shape, upholstered with "Vi-Down" or hair as preferred. They can be covered with fitted cases of customers own material, or finished in calico ready for use with detachable covers. Prices on application.

24

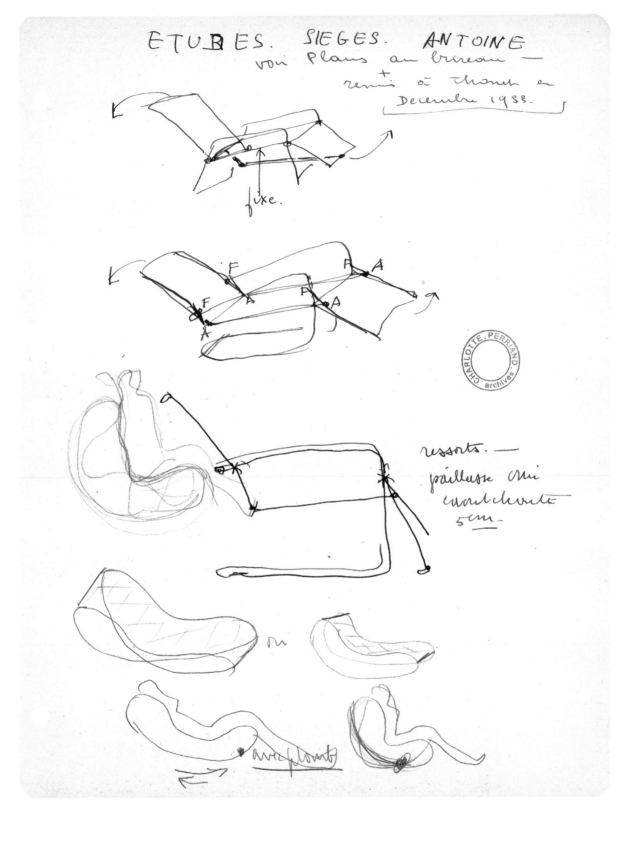

ETUDES. SIEGES. ANTOINE

voir Plans au bureau —
+
remis à Thonet en
Décembre 1988.

fixe.

F   F   A
F   A
F
A
A

ressorts. —
paillasse ou
caoutchouc
5cm.

ou

avec plomb

10 Oct 1979
Ch Perriand

Resumé – oscature apparente.
– penetration des pleins.
interieur et exterieur –
– (por portes coulissants
amovibles ou relevantes.
Haut des portes 1ᵐ 85.
– unité des materiaux
naturel – pour bien.
– Decors peinture ou laque
très sobre très delimité.

et pour
ou être par
rouleau ou
bandeau
transparent.

paravent limitant le
passage –

EN
M
O
D
E
R
N
E

(peur être remplacé par
meubles legers mais
attention il faut les imposer
de face – de dos

durant les fentes (suppression du m
le soir.

Rouleaux en materiaux naturels
ou — decors: tapisserie – tissu
ou en bois coulissants – peinture.

Pages from Japan notebook, 1940

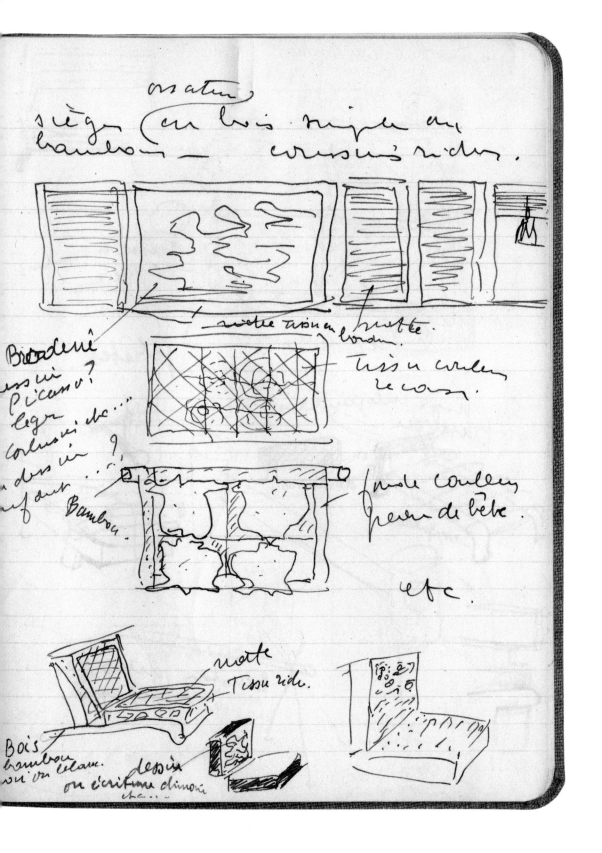

Perriand kept this notebook during her first year in Japan. It is both a journal and a record of her encounters with different craftspeople as she travelled the country. She made rough sketches in which you can see her working out how to use bamboo, which was a new material to her.

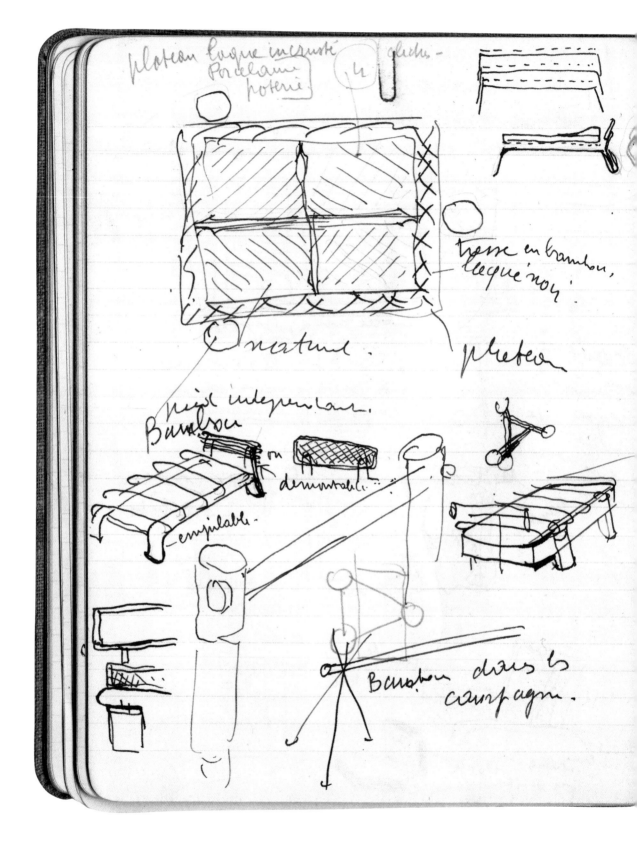

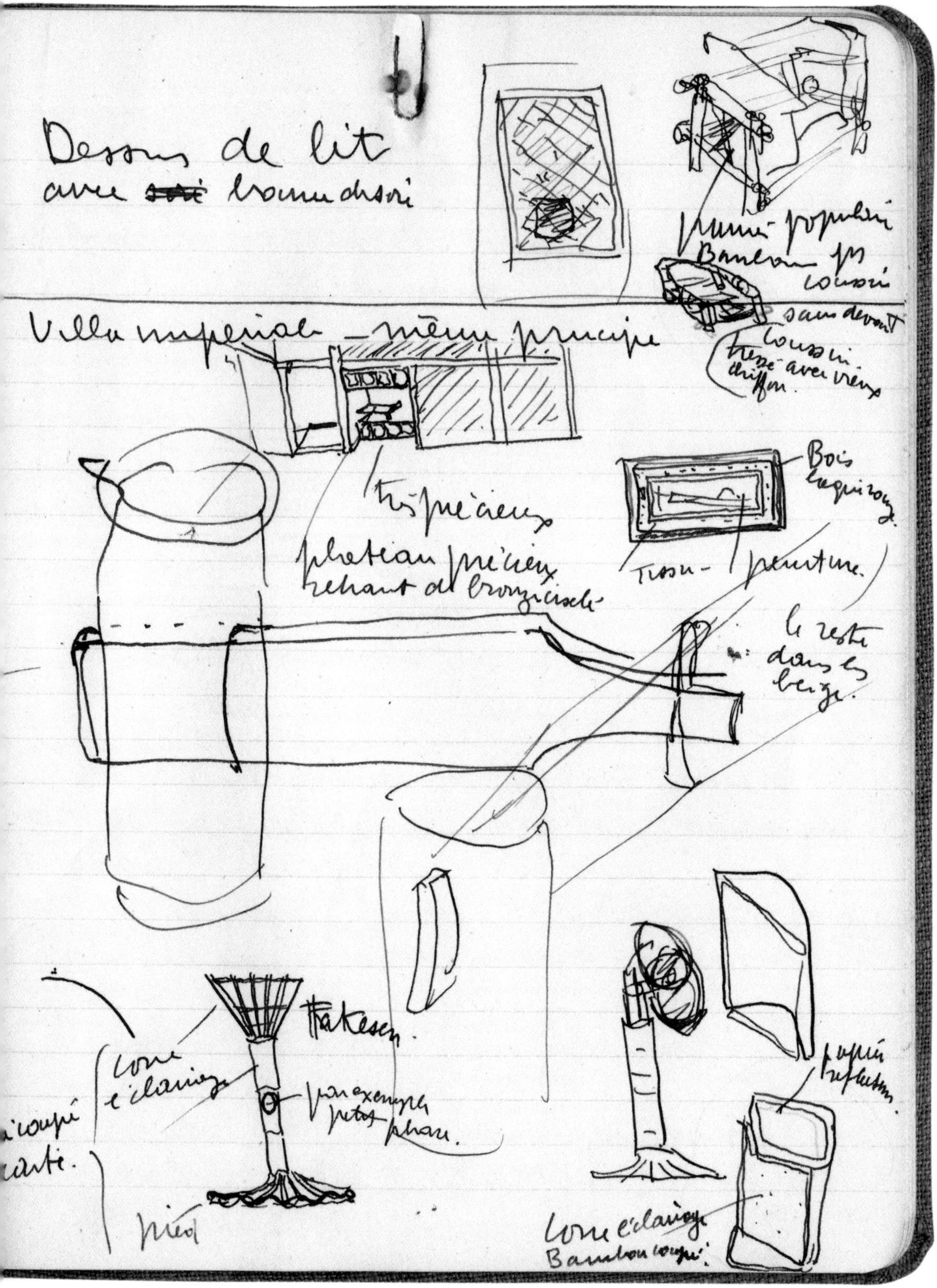

Dessous de lit
avec ~~son~~ bonne choson

Villa impérial — même principe

trois précieux
plateau précieux
rehaut de bronze doré

bois
laqué rouge

Tissu — peinture.

le reste
dans les
beige.

prune populaire
Bandou pour
coussin

sans devant
coussin
tissu avec vieux
chiffon.

Frakesen

par exemple
petit phare

pied

cone éclairage

papier
plastique

cone éclairage
Bambou coupé.

Mercredi 2.

Le matin : Villa impériale de Syugatium
: après midi promenade ville
— visite de temple.

les plateaux jaunes comme des nuages,
le meuble en biais coupe l'espace.

Bel situation — mais pure —
— beau jardin — un lac est composé
pour rappeler la mer ... la plage ...
ou un coin de mer et le mont Fuge.
le jardin composé de manière
à ce que les collines à l'infini
fassent partie intégrante du jardin ...
les buissons avec différentes plantes ...
couleurs différentes faisant jeux naturels sans
culbutes grosse importance, change le
paysage.

Bamboo

锦会时代`竹蔽

lettre limousé   Fécondité
                  Stabilité
                  prospérité
                           etc —
                  Bonheur.

en tissu velours relief . . . .
noir (ou nouveau c. à d. gris.)

plateau allumelté âme
            depuis foïeur

poésie   signature.

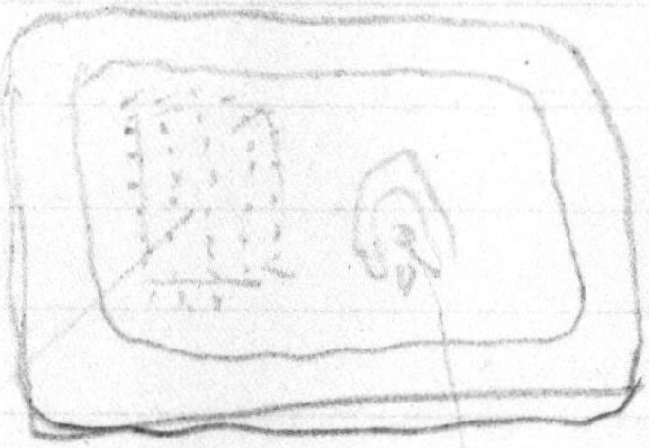

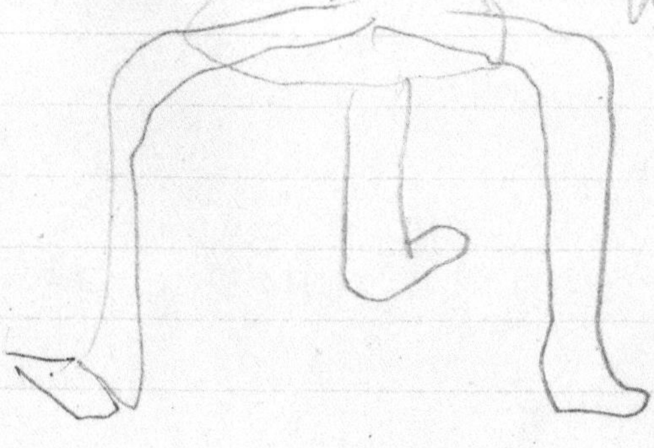

dessus plateau bois
            tripodi

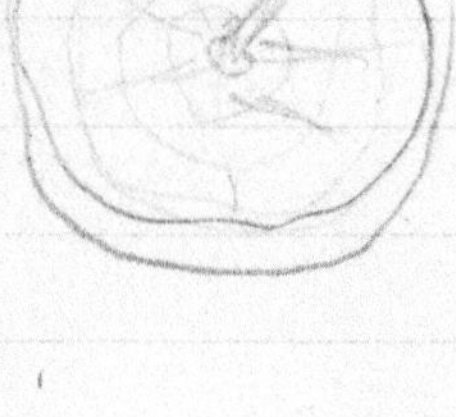

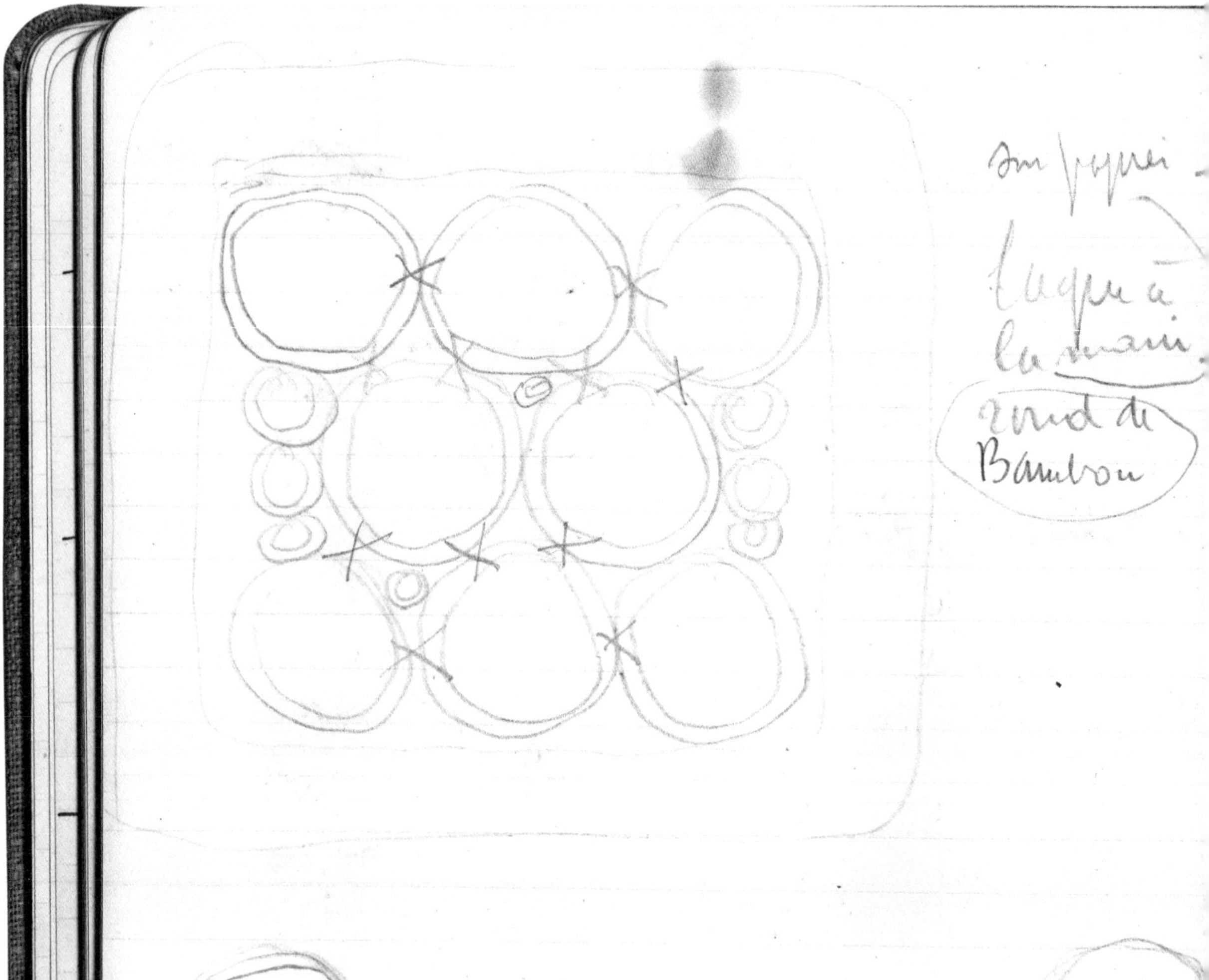

sur papier

laque à
la main
rond de
Bambou

laque transparente sur fond de
Bambou
laque noir

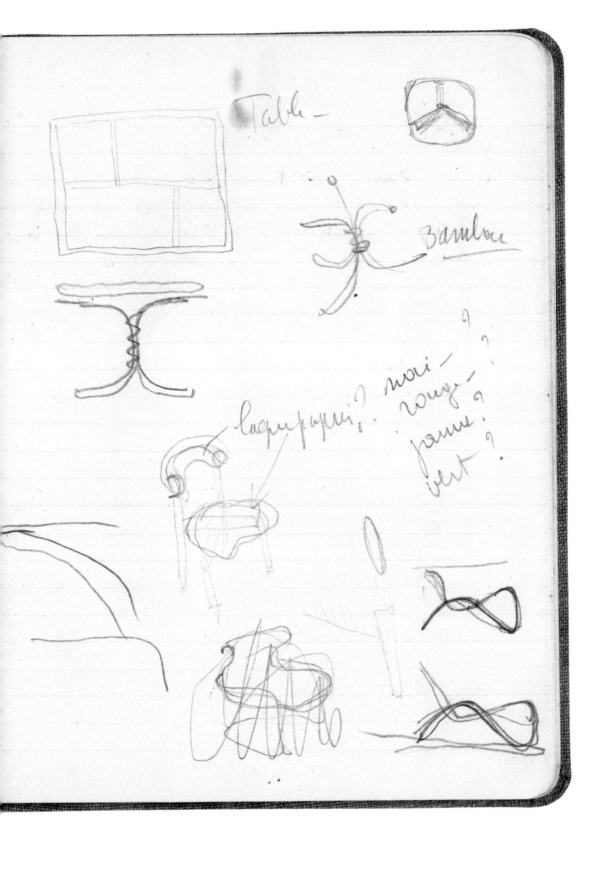

Table

Bambou

laquepapier? mari —
rouge —
jaune?
vert?

Exp. Kawaï Tokyo -
Faire dessus de Table

On voit

almaïte
noir.

Bois
terre.

— Vue.
chaise Bambou à

Avec Tissu papier faire coussin —

- Vu tapis Ridoweil - Tapisserie à Chissooka -

Jeudi 17.

Fêtes à :
- lutte en plein air des garçons
- un tambour. -
- exposition des travaux féminins -
- 1 côte chez des filles _ l'autre chez des garçons _
- exposition des mains des Denis _

le soir Dormir à Omsia.
Hôtel construit en 1930 trop luxueux.
mauvais - salle de bains avec cailloux
petit pont - l'eau chaude sort en
vapeur vers le petit pont et coule
ensuite dans le bouquon ___
- salle chambre intime et discrète_

Vendredi 18
Départ pour le Mt Fuji descente à.
bains - bronzer déjeuné syny attaqué
puis à travers la montagne (forêt)
arrivée au village de Nemba
puis de nuit à :
dormir hôtel japonais grande forêt
feu - grillés des mais_ bains _
chansons - batailles _ fumé

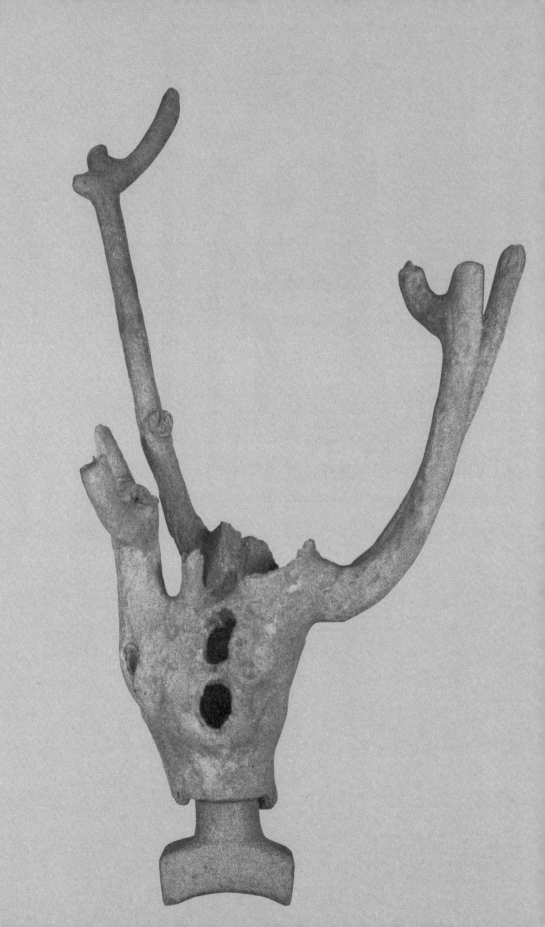

previous   Piece of wood shaped by the sea, 1933
above   Fernand Léger, *Nature morte, le mouvement à billes* (Still life with ball bearings), 1926
right   Charlotte Perriand and Alfred Roth at Place Saint-Sulpice, Paris, 1928

Several photographs of Perriand from the late 1920s show her wearing a necklace of ball bearings. She had
one in chrome and one that was gold-plated. Ball bearings, used in industrial machinery, were a symbol of modern
efficiency, as depicted in this painting of 1926 by the artist Fernand Léger. By wearing them around her neck,
Perriand was presenting herself as a quintessential modern woman. Perriand and Léger became good friends
and their work explored parallel themes.

above   *Bar sous le toit* (Bar under the roof), presented at the Salon d'Automne, 1927

right   Perspective rendering of *Bar sous le toit* in the Place Saint-Sulpice apartment–studio, Paris, 1927, published in *L'Art international d'aujourd'hui*, vol. 6, *Intérieurs* (1929)

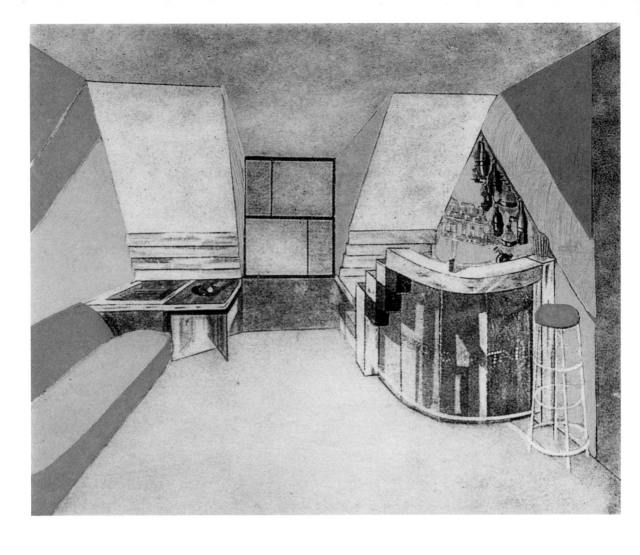

Perriand exhibited the *Bar sous le toit*, her breakthrough work, at the 1927 Salon d'Automne. In reaction to what she saw as the fussy, overly decorative and predominantly wooden designs of her peers, this was a recreation of the aluminium, chrome and glass room that she had originally built for her own attic apartment in Saint-Sulpice, Paris. After Perriand invited Le Corbusier to view her work, he was so impressed that he invited her to join his studio.

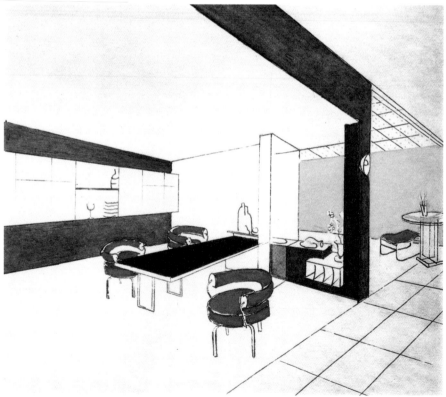

above   Dining room in the Place Saint-Sulpice apartment–studio, exhibited at the Salon des artistes décorateurs, 1928
below   Perspective rendering of the dining room in the Place Saint-Sulpice apartment–studio, Paris, published in
          L'Art international d'aujourd'hui, vol. 6, *Intérieurs*, 1929
right   Charlotte Perriand and Le Corbusier by the window at the *Bar sous le toit* (Bar under the roof), 1928

In 1927, in a former photographer's studio loft with vast windows and skylights, Perriand created a striking space for herself and her first husband, an Englishman called Percy Scholefield. Designed to be open plan and multifunctional, the apartment was bold and modern, grabbing the attention of all who visited. Her inventive solutions to make the studio feel more spacious included chimney stacks covered with mirrors and cabinets with sliding doors fitted into the sloping roof spaces. At the far end was the feature that so impressed Le Corbusier: the Bar under the roof.

above   Charlotte Perriand with Le Corbusier's hands holding a plate as a halo, 1928
right   *Travail et Sport* (Work and Sport), published in *Répertoire du goût moderne*, no. 2, fig. 20 (1929).
    Aerial view of the relaxation space transformed into an interior garden overlooking the other spaces,
    with shower and washbasin, behind the partition to which bunk beds are affixed

Pl. 20

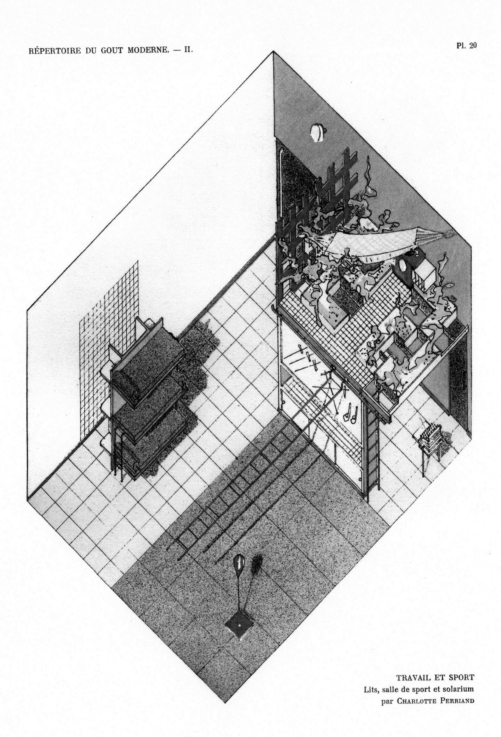

TRAVAIL ET SPORT
Lits, salle de sport et solarium
par CHARLOTTE PERRIAND

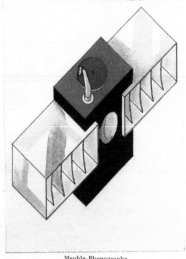

Meuble-Phonographe

Table Machine à écrire et siège

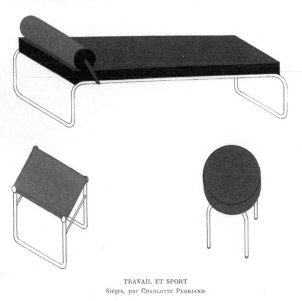

TRAVAIL ET SPORT
Sièges, par Charlotte Perriand

In this series of drawings from the interior design publication *Répertoire du goût moderne*, no. 2, Perriand imagined a multifunctional space for work, relaxation and exercise. As a keen sportswoman, her interest in the subject was personal. Her choice of steel and reinforced concrete allowed her to design a free plan that included a roof terrace for relaxation, a typewriter table as a workstation, and sliding bay windows to ensure the space was brightly lit.

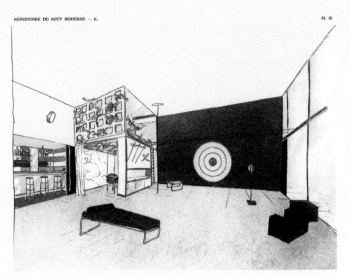

TRAVAIL ET SPORT
Vue sur la salle de sport et le bar, par CHARLOTTE PERRIAND

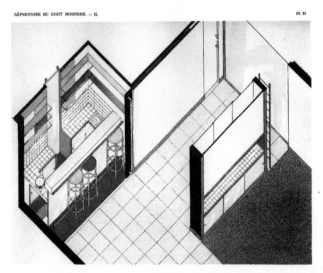

TRAVAIL ET SPORT
Salle à manger - cuisine - bar, par CHARLOTTE PERRIAND

left   *Travail et Sport* (Work and Sport), published in *Répertoire du goût moderne*, no. 2, fig. 22 (1929).
Phonograph cabinet, typewriter table and seat, bed with metal tubing, tubing-and-canvas stool, swivel stool
above   *Travail et Sport*, published in *Répertoire du goût moderne*, no. 2, fig. 19 (1929). Broad perspective drawing
below   *Travail et Sport*, published in *Répertoire du goût moderne*, no. 2, fig. 21 (1929). View of the bar-kitchen,
which opens on to the workspace and the exercise space via a sliding panel

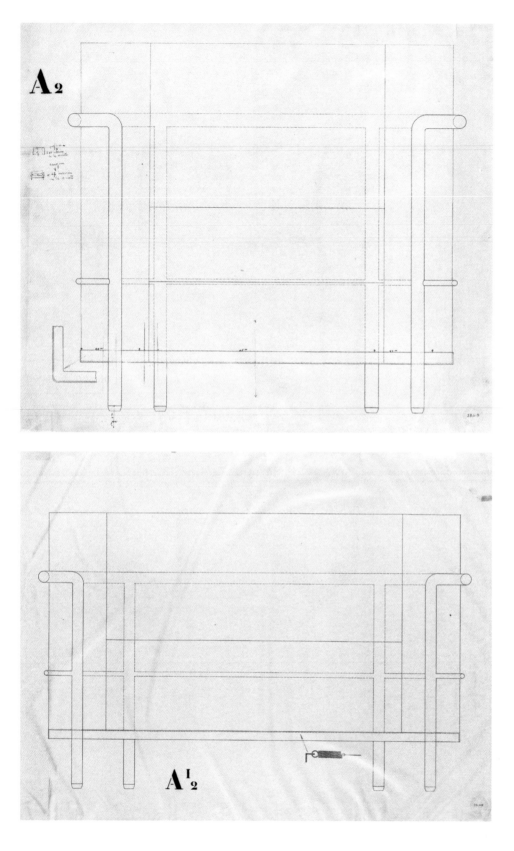

Manufacturing plans for the seat of the *Fauteuil grand confort*, large model, 1928

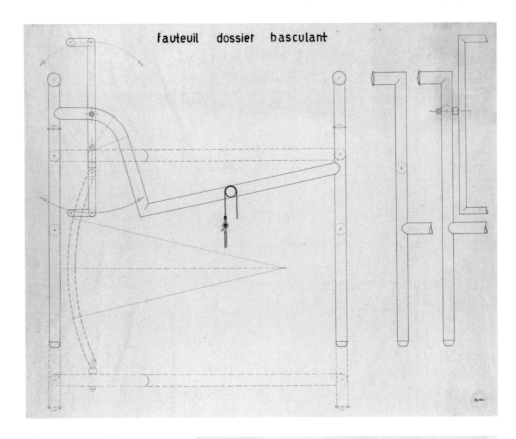

fauteuil dossier basculant

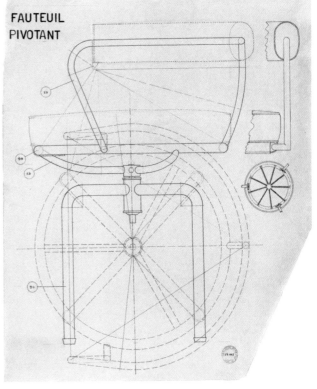

FAUTEUIL
PIVOTANT

above   Manufacturing plan for the *Fauteuil dossier basculant*, 1928
below   Manufacturing plan for the *Fauteuil pivotant*, 1927

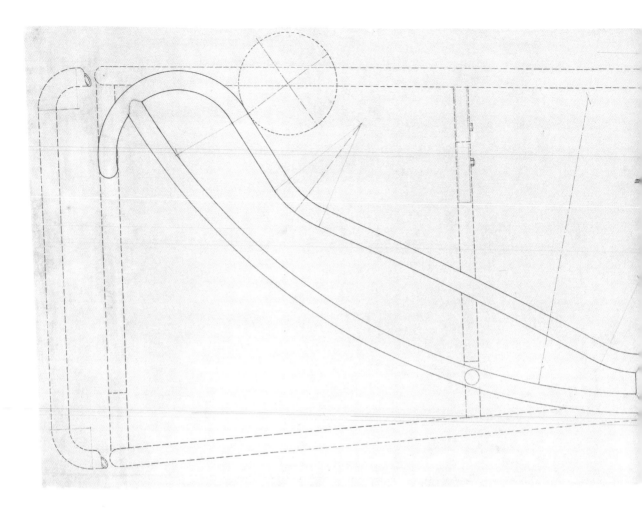

Manufacturing plan for the *Chaise longue basculante*, 1928

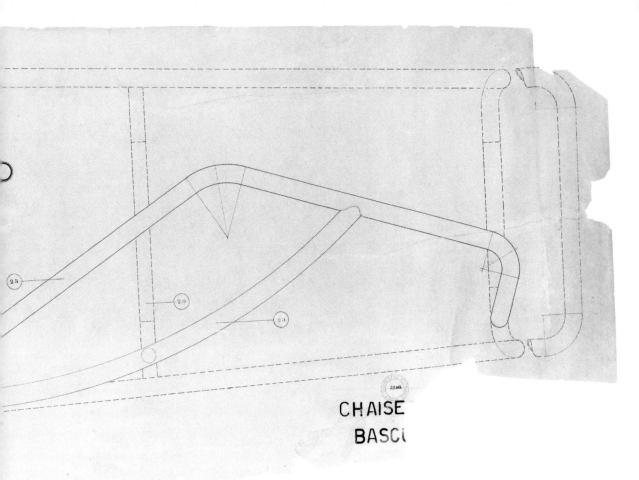

CHAISE
BASCU

The *Chaise longue basculante* is probably the most recognisable of Perriand's furniture designs. Various chaises longues already existed on the market, including Thonet's 1880 bentwood rocking chair and others for medical use, but this design combined adjustability and elegance. Perriand incorporated a base on which, unlike previous chairs of its type, a sliding cradle could adopt any position without the need for mechanical parts.

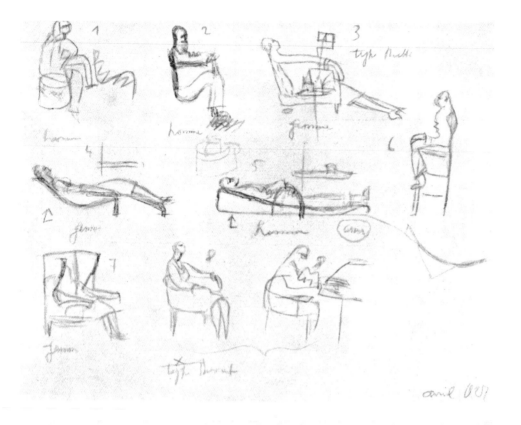

Mᵐᵉˢ Scholefield née Perriand,
MM. Jeanneret (C.-E.) dit le Corbusier et Jeanneret (A.-P.) Pl. unique

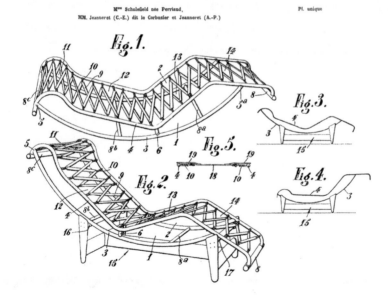

above   Le Corbusier, Study of different sitting positions, April 1927
below   Charlotte Perriand, Le Corbusier, Pierre Jeanneret, Patent drawing for *Chaise longue basculante*
        sliding system, 8 April 1929. Issued on 4 September 1929
right   Charlotte Perriand, Ergonomic study for chairs adapted to the positions of a mannequin, 1928

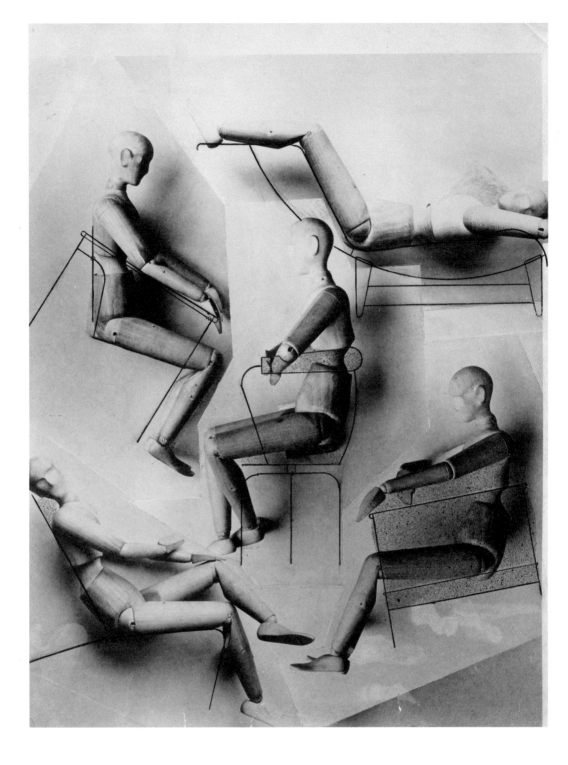

**B. 301
fauteuil
à
dossier
basculant**

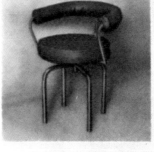

**B. 302
fauteuil
tournant**

**B. 304
tabouret
tournant**

**B. 303
chaise
tournante**

**B. 305
tabouret
de salle
de bain
recouvert
de tissu
éponge
inter-
changeable**

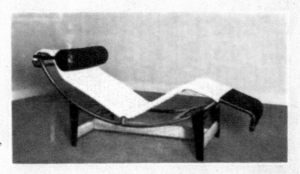

**B. 306
chaise longue
à position
variable**

Paris brochure presenting the models of the Le Corbusier, Pierre Jeanneret,
Charlotte Perriand range, published by Thonet, May 1931

MODÈLE { LE CORBUSIER
          P. JEANNERET
          CH. PERRIAND

Le Corbusier, Pierre Jeanneret, Charlotte Perriand, *Fauteuil grand confort*, large model, 1928

The *Fauteuil grand confort* encloses voluptuous leather cushions in a streamlined metal frame, which is tilted back slightly for comfort. The design draws on the form of an English club chair, but Perriand's use of an external metalwork structure was unique in furniture production at the time.

Advertising poster for Peugeot bicycles, 1922

Looking for a way to mass-produce her tubular-steel furniture, Perriand imagined that it could be manufactured by Peugeot, which made curved tubular-steel bicycle frames. However, the designers at Peugeot were baffled by her idea and discussions were short-lived.

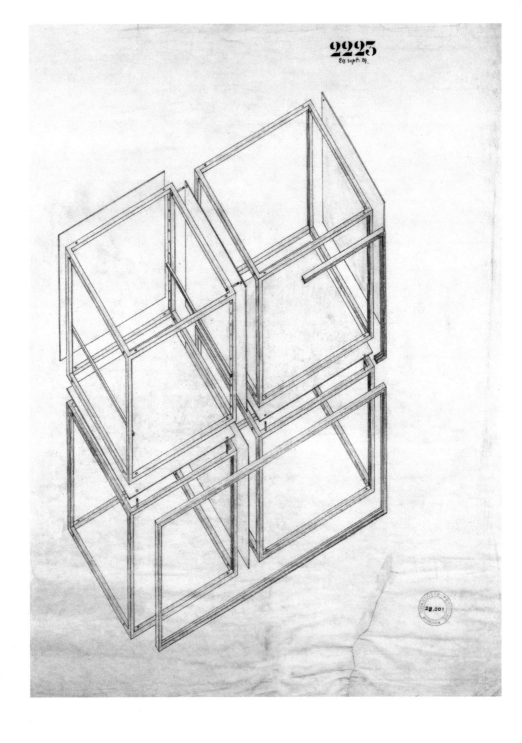

Research sketches for *casiers* (storage cabinets), 1929

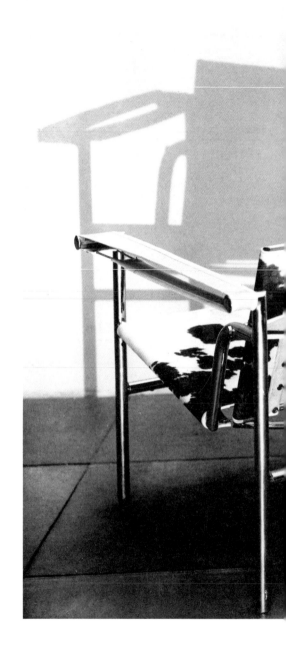

Le Corbusier, Pierre Jeanneret, Charlotte Perriand, *Siège à dossier basculant*, standard version, 1928

This was an updated version of the British Army campaign chair, which was portable and had leather straps for armrests. Called *basculant* because of its tilting back-support, the chair was ergonomically designed for sitting in an upright position, suitable for working. Its simple form is reduced to the bare essentials – a tubular-steel frame slung with leather.

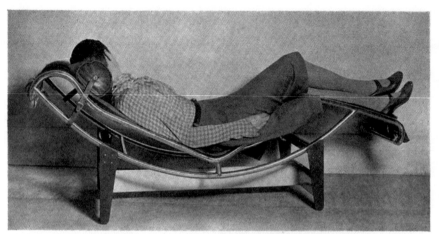

Metal Couch designed by Le Corbusier, Pierre Jeanneret and Charlotte Perriand

WOOD OR METAL?

A reply to Mr. John Gloag's article in our January issue by Charlotte Perriand who, as champion of new ideas, has adopted an original style of expressing them

METAL plays the same part in furniture as cement has done in architecture.

IT IS A REVOLUTION.

The FUTURE will favour materials which best solve the problems propounded by the new man :

I understand by the NEW MAN the type of individual who keeps pace with scientific thought, who understands his age and lives it : The Aeroplane, the Ocean Liner and the Motor are at his service ;

Sport gives him health ;

His House is his resting place.

WHAT IS HIS HOUSE TO BE?

Hygiene must be considered first : soap and water.

Tidiness : standard cupboards with partitions for these.

Rest : resting machines for ease and pleasant repose.

Beds : armchairs : chaises longues :

Office chairs and tables : Stools, some high and some low : Folding chairs.

The French word for furniture, " MEUBLES " comes from the Latin " mobilis " : meaning things that can be moved about.

The only things that come into this category are chairs and tables.

We have stated the problem ; now we must solve it. . . .

MATERIAL NOW IN USE AND MATERIAL THAT OUGHT TO BE USED.

WOOD : a vegetable substance, in its very nature bound to decay, it is susceptible to the action of damp in the air. " Central heating dries the air and warps wood." Since the war, we don't get dry wood any more : it is dried by artificial means, and inadequately.

Plywood : Composition wood :

These should be used for panels, mounted on a metal framework, and allowing for " play."

METAL : a homogeneous material of which certain alloys are liable to be affected by acids in the air :

In that case protection is afforded by oxidising, or by application of paint, Duco, etc. . . .

Cupboards of beaten sheet iron :

For chairs, metal " bicycle " tubes :

A bicycle weighs only 10 to 12 kilograms. The minimum of weight, the maximum of strength :

Autogenous welding = Δ

This process opens a vast field of practical possibilities.

The ratio between the weight necessary to ensure against breakage and the conditions of construction, in other words, the coefficient of security, would be about 6 in the case of metal, 10 in the case of wood. To be of the same solidity the wood would have to be 14 times as thick as metal:

THRUST
COMPRESSION } 14 times more in
FLEXION } wood than in steel

TECHNICAL CONCLUSIONS :
The EIFFEL TOWER could never have been made of Wood.
Metal is superior to wood ; reasons ?
The power of resistance in metal itself ;
Because it allows of mass production in the factory (lessens amount of labour required);
Because by means of the different methods of manufacture it opens out new vistas ; new opportunities of design ;
Because the protective coatings against toxic agencies not only lower the cost of upkeep, but have a considerable ÆSTHETIC value.
METAL plays the same part in furniture as cement has done in architecture.
IT IS A REVOLUTION.
ÆSTHETICS OF METAL.
Aluminium varnish, Duco,
Parkerisation, Paint,
all provide variety in the treatment of metal.
If we use metal in conjunction with leather for chairs, with marble slabs, glass and india-rubber for tables, floor coverings, cement,
vegetable substances,
we get a range of wonderful combinations and new æsthetic effects.
UNITY IN ARCHITECTURE and yet again
POETRY
A new lyric beauty, regenerated by mathematical science ;
Has produced a new kind of man who can love with fervour ; Orly's "Avion Voisin," a photograph of the Mediterranean, and "Ombres Blanches."
Even Mont Cervin is restored to a place of honour.

AS FOR THE PUBLIC :
OPERATION THEATRES :   Clinics, Hospitals :
Improve physical and moral health,
Nothing extraneous.
FASHION : Look at the shops (which serve the public taste).
They make metallised wood ;
They make imitation oak of metal ;
They have even planned a chair made of plywood, metal and india-rubber to imitate marble.
LONG LIVE COMMERCE.
THE MAN OF THE XXth CENTURY :
An INTRUDER ? Yes, he is, when surrounded by antique furniture, and NO, in the setting of the new Interior.
SPORT, *indispensable for a healthy life in a mechanical age.*
Modern mentality also suggests :
Transparency, reds, blues,
The brilliance of coloured paint,
That chairs are for sitting on,
That cupboards are for holding our belongings,
Space, light,
The Joy of creating and of living . . . in this century of ours.
BRIGHTNESS LOYALTY LIBERTY
in thinking and acting.
WE MUST KEEP MORALLY AND PHYSICALLY FIT.
Bad luck for those who do not.
CH. PERRIAND.

Comfortable chair, in steel treated with Duco, and leather. By Le Corbusier, Pierre Jeanneret and Charlotte Perriand·

279

'Wood or Metal?', published in *The Studio*, 97 (April 1929)

In January 1929, the British writer John Gloag, who was a member of the Design & Industries Association, published an article in the influential British magazine *The Studio*. It violently attacked the use of metal in furniture. Perriand responded by writing a polemical manifesto, entitled 'Wood or Metal?', in which she championed metal as a superior material and one that symbolised progress and the modern world.

5

Un equipement intérieur d'une habitation, presented at
the Salon d'Automne, 1929. Photomontage of the project

Le Corbusier, Jeanneret and Perriand presented this installation at the 1929 Salon d'Automne. It represented
a single-room apartment that was a masterclass in open-plan living and the radical use of space, and it celebrated
modern materials – metal and glass. The open-plan living area is separated from the kitchen, bathroom and
sleeping areas by metal storage cabinets. All the surfaces are chromed steel and glass, and the floor was originally
made of raw glass slabs laid on sand. To furnish the apartment, they chose the tubular-steel furniture they had
designed the previous year.

Le Corbusier, Pierre Jeanneret, Charlotte Perriand, Living room-dining room in
Un equipement intérieur d'une habitation, presented at the Salon d'Automne, 1929

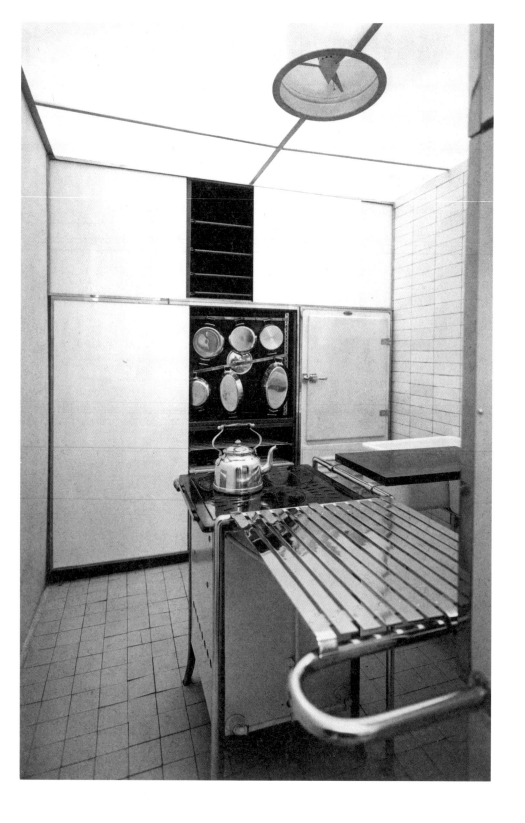

Le Corbusier, Pierre Jeanneret, Charlotte Perriand, *Un equipement intérieur d'une habitation*, presented at the Salon d'Automne, 1929

Le Corbusier, Pierre Jeanneret, Charlotte Perriand, Kitchen in *Un equipement intérieur d'une habitation*, presented at the Salon d'Automne, 1929

Le Corbusier, Pierre Jeanneret, Charlotte Perriand, Bedroom and bathing space in
Un equipement intérieur d'une habitation, presented at the Salon d'Automne, 1929

Le Corbusier, Pierre Jeanneret, Charlotte Perriand, Bathroom in *Un equipement intérieur d'une habitation*, presented at the Salon d'Automne, 1929

Siège pliant et empilable (Folding stackable chair), 1936

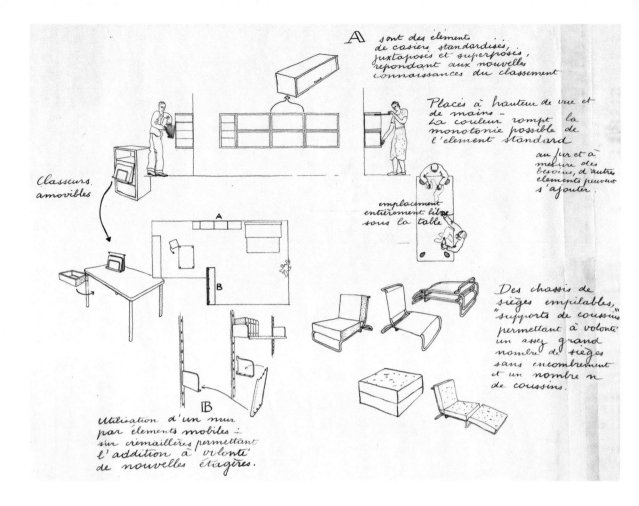

Drawing for the *Salle de séjour à budget Populaire* (Popular affordable living room) showing the *Siège pliant et empilable*, presented at the Salon des arts ménagers third Exposition de l'habitation organised by *L'Architecture d'aujourd'hui*, 1936

The tubular-steel furniture Perriand designed for Le Corbusier was not commercially successful, being produced in limited runs at high prices. However, Perriand still aimed to make her furniture affordable. This folding seat, modelled on a camping chair, was much simpler and cheaper to manufacture. It originally came with seat cushions, and formed part of a suite of furniture options designed for 'A living room on a budget', which she exhibited in 1936.

Mon vieux,

Nous ne ferons jamais du travail utile et sérieux – et continuer [destructeux] tout les deux, si nous continuons à parler sur le pied de guerre quand il s'agit d'architecture.

Si je délaisse Le Métier d'architecture pour me diriger sur des questions plus directement dans la vie c'est afin de voir plus clair dans ces problèmes, c'est aussi [le résultat] parce qu'il y avait un plafond, un mur dans notre travail.. dans notre esprit, parce que nous étions dans un cercle fermé – nous nous cristallisions le mur s'est fissuré, et au delà il y a tout un monde nouveau qui nous interesse au plus au point, car enfin le Métier d'Architecture c'est travailler pour l'homme, on ne peut travailler pour lui en l'ignorant, et en ignorant toutes les espèces d'hommes qui composent notre pays .... et en ignorant les points communs sur lesquels on peut les toucher ___

Nous nous sommes placés si loin en avant que nous en avons oublié la vie, son expression multiple dans la réalité.

above   Letter from Charlotte Perriand to Pierre Jeanneret, 1936
right   Two photographs of Pierre Jeanneret, c.1942

Perriand had a close working relationship with Le Corbusier's cousin and business partner Pierre Jeanneret, with whom she formed a lifelong friendship. In this letter to him, she shares her belief that architecture is a fundamentally social discipline. She underlines part of the sentence that reads: 'the Profession of Architecture is work in the service of humanity'. The two passport photos sent by Jeanneret six years later show, by contrast, the playful side of their correspondence. He has written on one, 'Without news. It's fun!', and on the other, 'With news'.

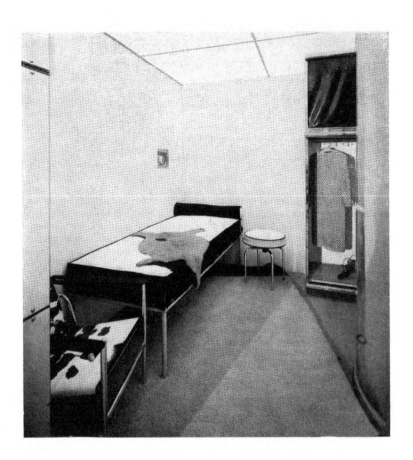

L'ÉLÉMENT BIOLOGIQUE :
LA CELLULE
DE 14 M² PAR HABITANT

(1930 — CONGRÈS DE BRUXELLES)

DÉDIÉ AUX « CONGRÈS INTERNATIONAUX D'ARCHITECTURE MODERNE »

L'ensemble des dessins relatifs à cette question a été publié dans « PLANS » 1931 :
1° logis pour célibataire ; 2° logis pour un couple ; 3° et 3 bis, idem ; 4° et 4 bis,
un couple et 1 ou 2 enfants ; 5° un couple et 2, 3 ou 4 enfants ; 6° un couple
et 3, 4, 5 ou 6 enfants ; 7° un couple et 5, 6, 7, 8, 9 ou 10 enfants. Ces travaux
ont été faits en collaboration avec Charlotte Perriand.

Le Corbusier, 'L'Élément biologique: la cellule de 14m² par habitant' (The biological
element: the 14m² module per inhabitant), *Éditions de L'Architecture d'aujourd'hui* (1935)

Between 1928 and 1930, a housing crisis prompted Perriand, Le Corbusier and Jeanneret to embark on a
project to calculate the minimum space required for a person to live comfortably. Although the official allowance
was defined as 7.5 square metres (81 square feet) per inhabitant, Perriand insisted on a minimum of 14 square
metres (150 square feet). To support her ideas, she designed various reconfigurable, multi-use modules called
cellules, organised around a collective living space.

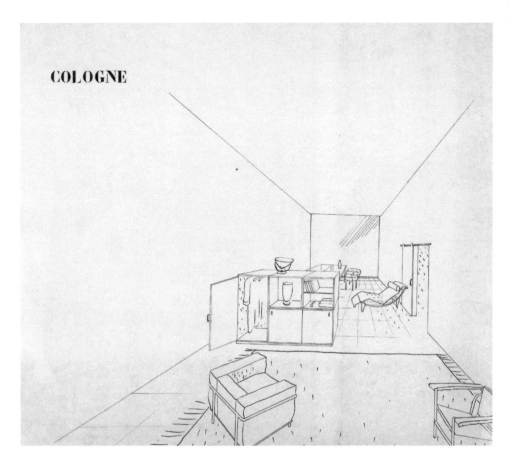

COLOGNE

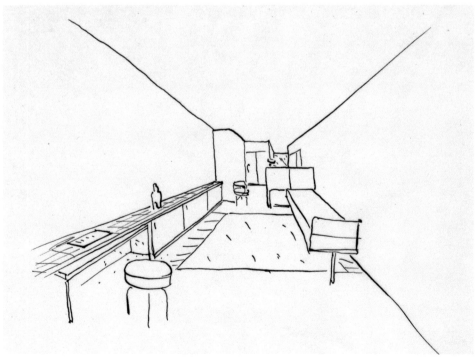

Perspective renderings for a 'minimum dwelling' module, 1931

Le Corbusier, Pierre Jeanneret, Charlotte Perriand, Perspective drawing
of the terrace of the Villa Martinez, Buenos Aires, October 1930

Le Corbusier entrusted Perriand with the design of a house for Julián Martinez, a lawyer in Buenos Aires. This was
an opportunity to put their system of metal cabinets, as tested in the Salon d'Automne, into full effect. The cabinets
were deployed as an architectural element, used as room dividers and lining the walls to keep the space as free
as possible. The house was to be raised off the ground, with a glazed facade in classic Corbusian style. The client
decided not to proceed, however, and the house was not built until the 1990s.

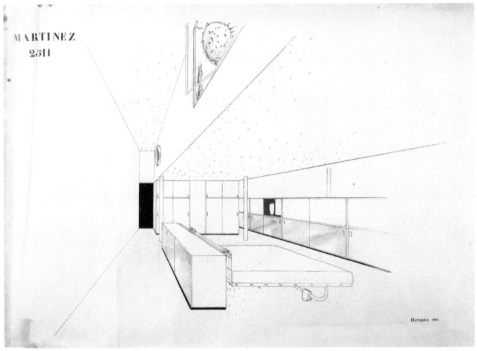

above   Le Corbusier, Pierre Jeanneret, Charlotte Perriand, Perspective drawing of
         the entrance and facade of the Villa Martinez, Buenos Aires, October 1930
below   Le Corbusier, Pierre Jeanneret, Charlotte Perriand, Perspective drawing of
         the ground-floor interior of the Villa Martinez, Buenos Aires, October 1930

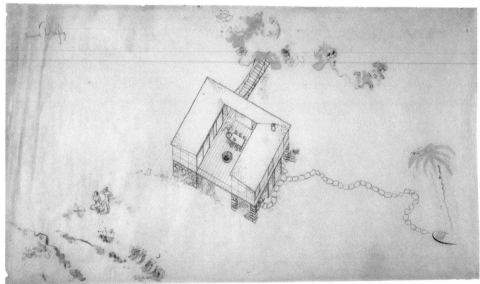

above   *Maison au bord de l'eau* (House by the water), 1934. Perspective rendering of the terrace
below   Bird's-eye view of *Maison au bord de l'eau*, with ground floor fitted out, 1934

Maison au bord de l'eau began as a competition entry for a modest weekend home, which Perriand adapted for
a wealthier clientele. It has three sides arranged around a terrace. The rooms have sliding doors opening on to the
terrace, which looks out to sea. Raising the house off the ground created space for parking and storage underneath.

Charlotte Perriand on a beach in Croatia, 1937

Fernand Léger, Charlotte Perriand, Le Corbusier, Albert Jeanneret, Pierre Jeanneret
and Matila Ghyka (left to right) in Athens, 1933

As Le Corbusier's associate, Perriand worked closely with the International Congress of Modern Architecture
(CIAM), which set the social agenda of the Modernist movement. In this photograph, she can be seen among her
peers, between Fernand Léger and Le Corbusier. The 1933 Congress had taken place on a cruise ship between
Marseille and Athens, and the key topic was the idea of the 'functional city'.

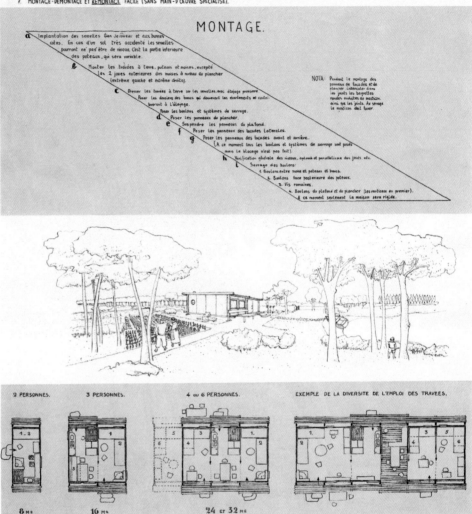

Charlotte Perriand, Pierre Jeanneret, Le Tritrianon, 1937. Systems for various layouts

In response to a competition in 1937 in the French architecture magazine *L'Architecture d'aujourd'hui*, Perriand worked with Jeanneret to design a weekend house she called Le Tritrianon. Also known as the Maison de l'agriculture, it comprised small huts where families of 'weekend farmers' could enjoy the outdoors and partake in gardening and growing crops. Each hut is surrounded by gardens that link to its neighbours. Perriand's concept was designed to be easily assembled and disassembled in a modular fashion. The design revolved around a central dwelling with a sleeping area and a room for 'services'. From here, different modules could be attached to enlarge the living area, according to the needs of the residents.

Pierre Jeanneret and Charlotte Perriand on board the sailing boat *Aventure*, 15 August 1938

nature and the synthesis of the arts

penny sparke
glenn adamson

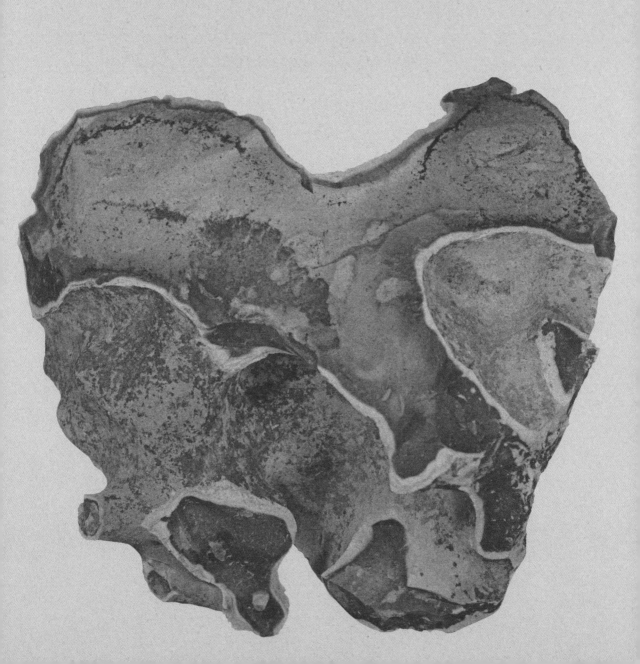

penny sparke

the natural world

previous   Piece of flint found in Maurienne, 1933
above   Charlotte Perriand looking out of the window of her studio in Montparnasse, c. 1934

Charlotte Perriand is probably best known for the work she undertook alongside Le Corbusier and Pierre Jeanneret on the iconic metal-framed *Grand confort* armchairs of 1928, the *Chaise longue basculante* of the same year, and the *Siège à dossier basculant* of 1929, all of which were exhibited together in a single-room flat in the 1929 Salon d'Automne in Paris. However, after she had abandoned her earlier fascination with furniture designed in the Art Deco style, largely executed in exotic woods, and before she joined Le Corbusier's studio in late 1927, Perriand had already undertaken several experiments with metal furniture on her own. The nickel-plated copper-framed stools in her *Bar sous le toit* (Bar under the roof), exhibited in 1927, and her chrome-tubing-framed *Fauteuils pivotants*, created for her apartment–studio in Place Saint-Sulpice, were among them. In 1929, the designer defended her commitment to the use of metal in furniture in a short text, published in the British journal *The Studio*. It was a riposte to an earlier article by John Gloag, who had attacked the idea.[1] In her text, Perriand contended that the 'NEW MAN' favoured metal because it was modern, hygienic, highly resistant, 'allows for mass production in the factory' and offered designers new aesthetic opportunities.[2]

However, in spite of her enthusiastic rhetoric, and although remaining in Le Corbusier's studio where, until 1937, she was in charge of its interiors work and a series of exhibitions, the early 1930s saw Perriand beginning to turn away from the industrialised world of metal and glass and towards the world of nature. As a marker of that shift, it was, according to Tim Benton, at around this time that she exchanged her necklace made of ball bearings for one made from seashells.[3] What was to become a very close relationship with the natural world was to manifest itself in several ways, from the inclusion of indoor plants in her early interiors; to her collections and photographs of rocks, pebbles, shells, driftwood and fossils; to her love of natural

materials, especially wood, leather and bamboo; and to her articulation, in many of her later furniture designs, of a free-form organic aesthetic. Not only did this volte-face mark an important moment in Perriand's career and work, given that nature is frequently seen as feminine (the words 'mother' and 'nature' have been used together for centuries), it also raises a question about the way in which this female designer constructed her own gendered identity.[4]

nature inside

Committed as Perriand was by the late 1920s to metal furniture, it is interesting to note that a 1928 photograph of the dining area in her Place Saint-Sulpice apartment – which featured a set of her *Fauteuils pivotants* positioned around a metal and glass table, a glass and chrome bar and a column clad with mirrored glass – depicted two large cacti and a vase of flowers adorning the surface of a shelving unit. That nature/culture combination was repeated in the designer's *Salle à manger 28*, shown at the

Dining room and living room space in *Maison au bord de l'eau* (House by the water), 1934. Prototype no. 1, presented by Louis Vuitton in a satellite exhibition of Design Miami, for Art Basel in Miami Beach, December 2013

1928 Salon des artistes décorateurs, in which the same table and chairs were accompanied, this time, by some potted trees and a large vase of tulips. In addition, an axonometric drawing of an interior named *Travail et Sport* (Work and Sport), which was published in *Répertoire du goût moderne* (Inventory of Modern Taste) in 1929 – a proposal containing some bunk beds, a sports room and a solarium – featured a roof garden, complete with flower beds, small trees, a trellis and a hammock. Even the Interior Design of a Dwelling exhibit at the 1929 Salon d'Automne, which was dominated by the items of metal-framed furniture mentioned above, was also enhanced by the presence of several vases of flowers.

The simplest interpretation of the presence of plants and flowers in these interiors is that they were added as last-minute decorative elements to offset the otherwise hard, industrial appearance of the setting and its components in the photographs that were taken of them. A deeper reading of that nature/culture combination might claim that it denoted a continuity with the past, especially with the Victorian era and its commitment to bringing live nature indoors. Trained as a furniture designer in the *ensemblier* tradition at the École de l'Union centrale des arts décoratifs in Paris, Perriand was clearly very comfortable creating whole interiors as well as individual items. Arguably, in her role as an interior decorator/designer, she was following a gendered path that had started in the mid-nineteenth century with the emergence of the notion of the so-called 'separation of the spheres', an ideological construct that was rooted in the idea that middle-class men went to work outside the home while women remained inside it with responsibility for everything within it, including the appearance of its interiors. The widespread presence of plants – from palms to ferns to aspidistras – in nineteenth-century middle-class homes represented a recognition, by women at home, of the need to maintain a link with the natural world in urban settings; of the link between nature and God; of the importance of the natural world

to the education of children; and of the therapeutic and well-being effects of indoor nature. Although, along with several of her fellow modernists, Perriand rejected the softness and luxuriance of palms and ferns for the hard, sculptural forms of cacti, arguably, on one level, she was nevertheless sustaining an earlier tradition of feminine intervention in interior settings.[5]

However, at no time in her career did Perriand present herself as a female homemaker. Although her mother was a seamstress and the designer was undoubtedly skilled in several 'feminine accomplishments' (when she first approached Le Corbusier to work in his studio he remarked that he didn't need an embroiderer), her relationship with nature arguably took a different route – one that was also followed by many of the male artists, designers and architects with whom she mixed.

found objects/dead nature

When, in 1934, Perriand produced some sketches of a *Maison au bord de l'eau* (House by the water), which was conceived for a competition for the design of a cheap holiday home, organised by the magazine *L'Architecture d'aujourd'hui* (The Architecture of Today), she was not embracing nature as an amateur housewife but rather as a highly professional architect–designer who was not defined by her gender and who saw herself as an equal to the men with whom she was working. Inspired by traditional Japanese architecture, the design won second prize but was never built. It has been described by Jacques Barsac as 'a system for contemplating nature'.[6] In the design, nature was represented by the widespread presence of wood (floors, walls, ceilings, furniture and so on), which defined a simple structure surrounding a courtyard that was open at one end. The most dramatic use of that material was represented by the stools, which surrounded a table positioned in the open space. Made from roughly hewn trunks of trees, they had a simple, rustic, vernacular feel to them. No longer suggesting that design should be made available to everyone through factory production but, rather, through simple hand-making as had been done for centuries, they marked an important departure for Perriand.

In a 2013 construction of the House by the water, made by Louis Vuitton from Perriand's sketches, open shelving positioned behind the table was home to some beach finds, among them a dried starfish, a fish's jawbone and some shells. This was one of the first manifestations of the designer's love of beachcombing and her practice of displaying the 'magical' finds that she came across.

Perriand loved being outdoors, especially on beaches and in the mountains. The latter stemmed from childhood holidays in Savoie, visiting her grandparents. The former grew from spending time with Jeanneret (and occasionally Fernand Léger) on the beaches near Dieppe where they would collect beach finds like those displayed in the House by the water. The appeal of these objects undoubtedly lay in the way in which they had been formed by the forces of nature; their irregular forms; the fact that the act of removing them from their original context transformed them into objects for contemplation (along the lines of objets trouvés); and that they belonged to the world of the everyday rather than the more rarefied one of conventional fine art.[7]

Perhaps the fact that these mementos of living nature were no longer alive also held an attraction. Unlike the plants that inhabited the Victorian household, which needed constant attention, these dead objects did not exert any agency and succumbed totally to the controlling hands and minds of artists. The French term nature morte, the equivalent of 'still life' in English, has a resonance in this context, denoting, as it does, that once artists had captured the world of nature, its life was taken away from it. Arguably, this way of relating to the natural world was a characteristically modernist strategy, one with which Perriand and her companions happily aligned themselves.

The term Art Brut was coined to describe the work that emerged from the walks on the beach. While Léger integrated the beach finds into several of his artworks – among them a gouache study, Silex jaune sur fond beige (Yellow flint on a beige background), of 1932 – Perriand took photographs of them and of natural imagery more generally. One in particular, Black locust logs of 1933, recalled the stools in the House by the water. While her photograph Galet sur le sable (Pebble on the sand) of 1935 depicts a stone in situ on the beach, its lyrical form mirrored by the shapes and lines formed by the sea rolling over the sand, another image from 1933, this time of a fish skeleton, titled Arête de Poisson (Fish Bone), is a more abstracted study. That link between nature and abstraction was a key modernist strategy, which sat alongside the association that was also made between machines and abstraction. The former produced an organic aesthetic and the latter a geometric one. Nature, in this context, was considered a source of inspiration, something that could be used to artistic ends and that served to sever the link between art and its earlier bourgeois connotations.

Le Corbusier also engaged in beachcombing and took inspiration from the natural world.[8] According to Tim Benton, 'by 1928 Le Corbusier began to collect objets trouvés ... systematically, for exhibition in his and his clients' houses and for inclusion in his paintings.'[9] In her essay 'Nature revisited in the 1930s: making their own way in the open air', Gladys C. Fabre claims that in his approach to the natural world Le Corbusier (and Léger) 'oppose[d] the masculine and feminine in their works', while Perriand 'took the Human into account in its entirety', thereby reinforcing the female designer's essentially humanist, rather than gendered, view of the world.[10] Benton has reminded us that Le Corbusier's books – Urbanisme of 1925 and La Ville Radieuse of 1935 – included illustrations of natural forms, and that it was in the period 1926–36 that the architect abandoned his mechanistic approach in

favour of a more organic one.[11] The impact on his architecture was visible from the 1940s onwards. Whether it was Le Corbusier who influenced Perriand or vice versa is lost to history. Ultimately, however, the two architects took their affinity with nature in different directions, the former using what he understood to be underlying order to transform his architecture (the roof of the chapel at Ronchamp is, for example, said to be based on an inverted crab's shell), while Perriand's approach was more sensorial than intellectual, revelling as she did in the texture of natural materials and the beauty of its forms. 'Wood is made for caressing,' she wrote, adding that, sometimes the top, left in its rough form, of a sliced trunk loses the eye in a 'warm strangeness'.[12]

natural materials

In 1935, Perriand exhibited an interior, titled *Maison du jeune homme* (House for a young man), at the Exposition Universelle in Brussels. It contained a painting by Léger based on a study of aloes, some of the designer's photographs and some shelving with yet more beach finds displayed on it. The interior also contained a rustic-looking oak armchair with a rush seat and back (Armchair No.21). This was among the first fabricated furniture items through which Perriand expressed her love of natural materials as part of a vernacular tradition. Although she had used pony skin and leather on the metal furniture items created with Le Corbusier and Jeanneret, she was now

Sandstone on a beach in Normandy, 1935

referencing objects and materials from a pre-industrial past that were so simple, so universal and so timeless that they could be seen as 'modern' in the mid-1930s. While there was a level of revivalism in this simple design, it looked at home alongside the Léger painting and the *Fauteuil pivotant*. For Perriand, simple, artisan-manufactured objects made of natural materials evoked the timeless designs of the agrarian working class, with which she felt a close affinity.[13]

Between 1934 and 1935, the designer had undertaken a study of vernacular architecture in the Jura Mountains and the region of Savoie, which she knew well. It clearly informed her venture into furniture made from oak, ash, fir, mahogany and pine – woods that were both widely available and inexpensive. Examples of her neo-vernacular designs included several little three-legged stools, modelled on shepherd's stools and milking stools, which she created over a number of decades, and some slatted benches, which she designed through the 1950s and 1960s. These included a bench for the middle-income apartments in the Les Arcs ski resort in the Tarentaise Valley – one of Perriand's last projects, which she worked on from 1967 to 1989. When she visited Japan in the years of the Second World War, Perriand's fascination with natural materials drew her to experiment with bamboo, realising some notable designs including a new version of the *Chaise longue basculante*, previously made in metal.

Charlotte Perriand's studio in Montparnasse with the six-sided free-form table, 1938

natural forms

Perriand's close relationship with the natural world extended beyond her sensorial response to natural materials for their own sake to an interest in free form, which she borrowed from natural objects. Inspired by the random shapes of the pieces of driftwood and other jetsam that she found on the beach, she designed many asymmetrical and irregular furniture items – especially tables. An early example – a pine table with six sides of different lengths and a thick wooden top with bevelled edges – was created for her studio in Montparnasse in 1938. While rustic in appearance, it was also practical, as it could seat more people around it than a square or rectangular table might have been able to. Its three legs also permitted its sitters more freedom. Although Perriand worked very intuitively, her free-form tables were considered from an ergonomic perspective, too, which imbued them with a level of rationalism. Many more free-form designs emerged over subsequent decades, from the highly ergonomic wooden Boomerang desk of 1938 – designed for Jean-Richard Bloch, the editor in chief of the *Ce Soir* newspaper – to a coffee table made from an untreated tree slab in 1941, to an oak desk created for the Hotel le Doron in Méribel-les-Allues in 1947.

From the mid-1930s onwards, Charlotte Perriand's relationship with nature drove her work forward in a variety of ways. She developed the lessons she learnt from her modernist engagement with the 'found object' into a highly individualistic approach to the design of architecture, interiors and furniture. Most importantly, she was able to align it with her strong political convictions, which were rooted in a commitment to democratic design and in a belief in the power of design, in alignment with nature, to bring a sense of well-being to everyone. Her approach was largely intuitive and sensorial, but it also embraced a level of practicality and pragmatism, a combination that is often seen – albeit stereotypically – as a feminine skill. However, Perriand's gendered identity as a designer was perhaps less important to her than her political mission, and she clearly did not consider that either she or her work were different from, or in any way inferior to, that of her male colleagues. Also, while her position within modernism meant that she saw nature as a source to be used, whether literally or metaphorically, her deep sense of empathy with the natural world anticipated the current era, in which designers are seeking to loosen the control that humankind had over nature in the past and to develop a more equal relationship with it.

1   Charlotte Perriand, 'Wood or Metal?', *The Studio*, 97 (April 1929), 278–9. Reproduced in Jacques Barsac, Sébastien Cherruet and Pernette Perriand (eds), *Charlotte Perriand: Inventing a New World* (Paris: Foundation Louis Vuitton and Gallimard, 2019), 78.

2   Ibid., 79.

3   Tim Benton, 'Modernism and Nature', in *Modernism 1914–1939: Designing a New World*, ed. Christopher Wilk (London: V&A Publications, 2006), 320.

4   See Susannah Hagan, *Taking Shape: A New Contract between Architecture and Nature* (Oxford: Architectural Press, 2001), 19–21; and Kate Soper, *What is Nature? Culture, Politics and the Non-human* (London: John Wiley and Sons, 1995).

5   For more detail about modernist architects' uses of indoor nature, see Penny Sparke, *Nature Inside: Plants and Flowers in the Modern Interior* (London and New York: Yale University Press, 2021), 69–85.

6   Katy Donoghue, 'Charlotte Perriand and Louis Vuitton: La Maison au bord de l'eau', *Whitewall* (1 December 2013), www.whitewall.art/design/charlotte-perriand-louis-vuitton-la-maison-au-bord-de-leau [Accessed 20 August 2020].

7   '*Objet trouvé* comes from French, where it literally means "found object". The term entered English during the early twentieth century, a time when many artists challenged traditional ideas about the nature of true art. Surrealists and other artists, for instance, held that any object could be a work of art if a person recognised its aesthetic merit. "Objet trouvé" can refer to naturally formed objects whose beauty is the result of natural forces as well as to man-made artifacts (such as bathtubs, wrecked cars, or scrap metal) that were not originally created as art but are displayed as such.' *Merriam-Webster* dictionary (2011), merriam-webster.com/dictionary/objet%20trouvé [Accessed 4 November 2020].

8   See Niklas Maak, *Le Corbusier: The Architect on the Beach* (London: Hirmer, 2007).

9   Benton (2006), 319.

10   Gladys C. Fabre, 'Nature revisited in the 1930s: making their way in the open air', in Barsac, Cherruet and Perriand (2019), 92.

11   Tim Benton, 'Le Corbusier and Nature with Tim Benton' (National Trust Salon, 18 June 2020).

12   Charlotte Perriand, *Charlotte Perriand: A Life of Creation* (London: Monacelli Press, 2000), 106.

13   Benton (2006), 318.

Six-sided free-form table in her studio in Montparnasse, 1938

In the late 1930s, Perriand turned decisively away from metal manufacture in favour of heavy wooden furniture. This was a significant statement at a time when the Machine Age had become associated with industrial-scale warfare, the rise of fascism and the atrocities of the Spanish Civil War. Influenced by her study of natural forms, Perriand designed a number of 'free-form' tables. These were not just organic shapes, but also highly considered designs for social gatherings. The six-sided pine table, originally designed for her studio in Montparnasse, Paris, allowed more seated guests than a rectangular one, and the three table legs left more space for their knees.

Boomerang desk for Jean-Richard Bloch, 1938, and *Fauteuil pivotant*, 1927.
In back, wall-mounted storage cabinet, 1938

Jean-Richard Bloch seated at the Boomerang desk by Charlotte Perriand, 1938

One of Perriand's most significant 'free-form' pieces was the desk she designed for Jean-Richard Bloch, editor of the French newspaper *Ce Soir*. Named after a boomerang because of its shape, the curved top was highly functional, designed for group editorial meetings. Just by swivelling in his chair behind the boomerang, Bloch could turn to face each member of the team without imposing any hierarchy.

above   Ergonomic drawing of the Boomerang desk, 1938
below   Charlotte Perriand, Fernand Léger, Pablo Picasso, Manifesto coffee table for Jean-Richard Bloch, 1937

above   Pablo Picasso, *The Dream and Lie of Franco*, plate 2, 1937
below   Joan Miró, *Aidez l'Espagne* (Help Spain) poster, 1937

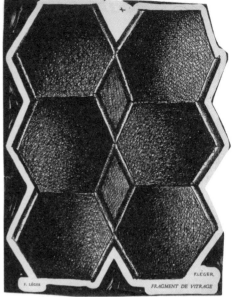

above   Fernand Léger, *Tire-bouchon* (Corkscrew), 1933 (left)
          Fernand Léger, *Fragment de vitrage* (Fragment of glass), 1933 (right)
below   Charlotte Perriand, Fernand Léger, Pablo Picasso, Manifesto coffee table for Jean-Richard Bloch, 1937

In 1937, Perriand had designed a coffee table for Jean-Richard Bloch. As the editor of a Communist Party newspaper, he took an anti-fascist position in his coverage of the Spanish Civil War. This table featured four zinc etching plates used to print two drawings by Fernand Léger and Pablo Picasso's diptych *The Dream and Lie of Franco*, which denounced the Spanish dictator's atrocities. The table, now lost, was a statement of Perriand's stance during her most politically active period.

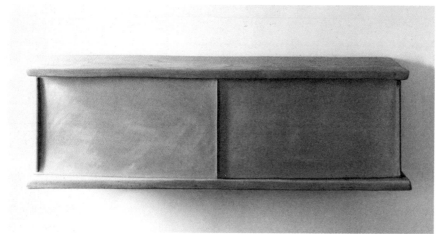

above   *Potence pivotant* (Pivoting stem) wall-mounted light, 1939
below   Free-form sideboard with sliding doors, 1939

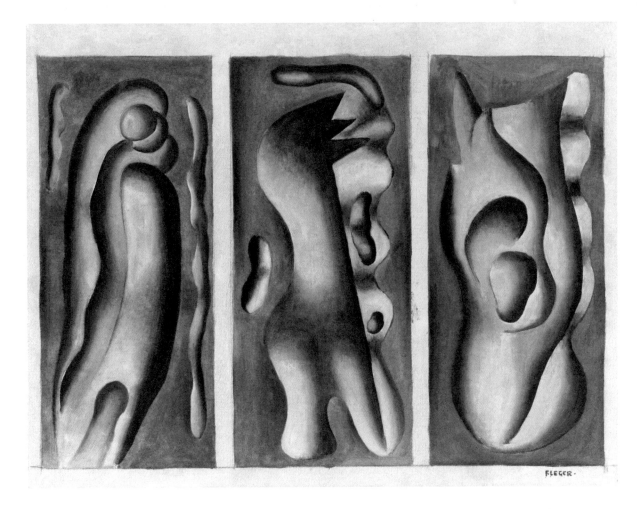

Fernand Léger, *Queues de comètes, étude pour un paravent* (Comet tails, study for a screen), c.1930.

In the early 1930s, the painter Fernand Léger was, like his friend Perriand, absorbed by natural forms. This triptych study for a room divider appears to draw on his observation of flints and other rock forms.

F.L.32

Fernand Léger, *Silex* (Flint), 1932

Charlotte Perriand on the beach with a friend, c. 1935

Charlotte Perriand on the beach, c. 1935

Around 1925, the Surrealists highlighted the importance of natural objects found outdoors as sources of inspiration for their art. From 1930 onwards, Perriand began photographing found objects with the same motivation. Often she would photograph these in a simple, documentary way. She took many pictures of animal skeletons, tree trunks, pebbles, rocks and ice sheets, using them as sources of inspiration for her furniture and architecture designs.

clockwise from top left
Ice sheet held by two hands, Fontainebleau Forest, 1935
Ice sheet held by four hands, Fontainebleau Forest, 1935
Ice sheet held by two hands, Fontainebleau Forest, 1935
Ice sheet held by two hands, Fontainebleau Forest, 1935

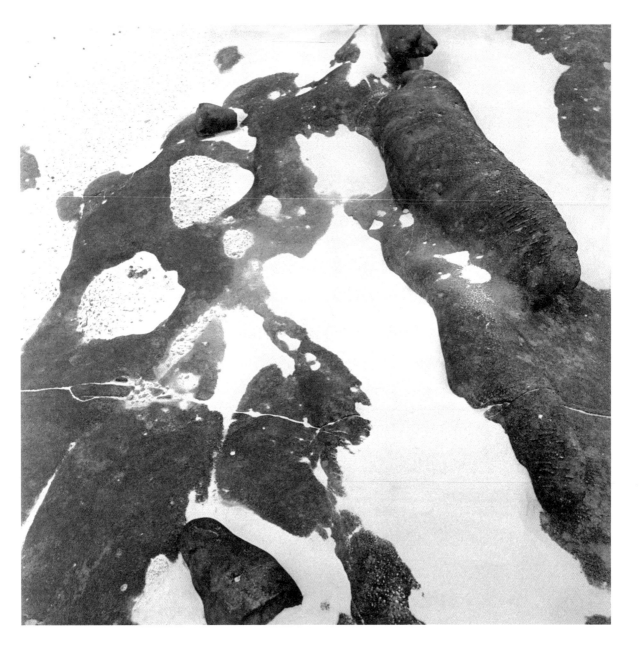

above   Snow on the stone I, Fontainebleau Forest, 1935
right   Snow on the stone II, Fontainebleau Forest, 1935

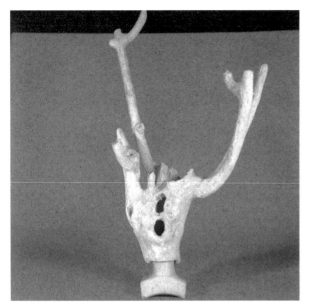 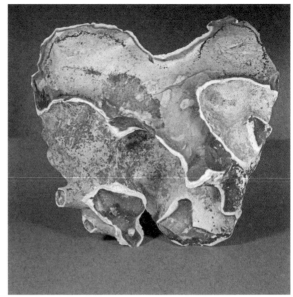

clockwise from top left
Piece of wood shaped by the sea, 1933
Piece of flint found in Maurienne, 1933
Piece of flint, 1933
Piece of flint shaped by the sea, 1933

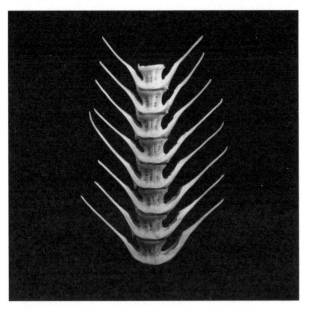
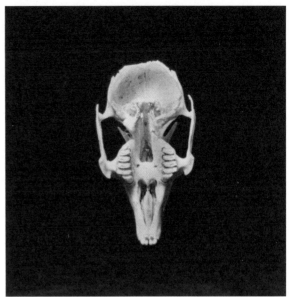
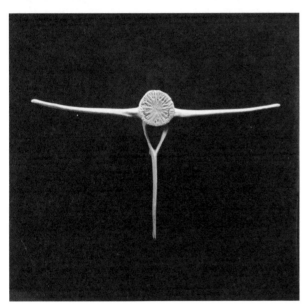
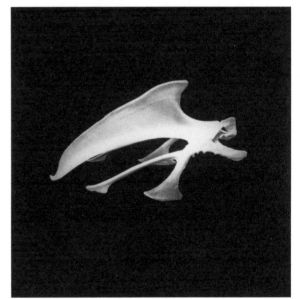

clockwise from top left
Fish vertebrae, 1933
Animal skull, 1933
Chicken carcass, 1933
Fish bone, 1933

51

Sandstone from the Bourron quarry, 1935

above   Sandstone on a Normandy beach, 1935
below   Burnt wood, Corsica, 1937

clockwise from top left
Cut locust tree, Fountainebleau Forest, 1933
Trunk of Saphora japonica, Paris, 1933
Cut locust tree, Fountainebleau Forest, 1933
Cut locust tree, Fountainebleau Forest, 1933

glenn adamson

perriand's handmade modernism

previous   Armchair with rush seat, model no. 21, 1935. Later issued by L'Équipement de la Maison and BCB

above   Study room in the *Maison du jeune homme* (House for a young man), Exposition Universelle, Brussels, 1935

Modernism was not meant to be handmade. Not at first, anyway: the idea was to bring principles of rigour and efficiency to mass production, improving the material culture of the masses. It didn't work out as planned. The bold abstract furniture of Gerrit Rietveld, intended as the building blocks of a brave new world, were no more widely distributed than the paintings of Piet Mondrian, his colleague in the De Stijl movement. At the Bauhaus, designs for textiles by Anni Albers, for chairs by Marcel Breuer, for ceramics by Otto Lindig, all remained at prototype stage; photographs of objects from the school's metal shop were actually doctored to make it look as if they had been machine-made.[1]

Charlotte Perriand had a similar experience. The famous tubular-steel designs that she developed in collaboration with Pierre Jeanneret and Le Corbusier, in the late 1920s, were produced in frustratingly limited numbers by their manufacturing partner, Thonet Frères. (They had initially hoped to work with Peugeot's bicycle division, a more industrialised operation, but were turned down.) Despite Perriand's best efforts to manage the relationship, she and her allies faced an insoluble conundrum: unless they could get their objects mass-produced, they would never be able to achieve economies of scale; but as long as their designs remained expensive – at Thonet, their steel furniture was made in what were literally called 'luxury runs' – they would inevitably struggle to achieve mass acceptance.

The usual way of continuing this story is to leap ahead to the 1950s, when American companies like Herman Miller and Knoll did at last bring modernist forms to a mass market. But this skips a major chapter of the story, one that might be described as the era of 'handmade modernism'. I borrow this term from the scholar Gökhan Karakuş, whose particular research focus is design in Turkey. There, cosmopolitan-minded architects and sculptors forged partnerships with artisans, notably at the Kare Metal Company, which laboriously reshaped plumbing pipes and construction rods into the country's first domestically produced modernist furniture. The results, as Karakuş notes, have 'the simplicity and directness that one might expect of craftsmanship' but were made 'to the designs of individuals who had a very advanced understanding of abstract sculpture'.[2] As this example begins to suggest, not only the early prototyping of modernism in the 1920s, but also the less well-known story of the style's global proliferation over the succeeding decades – in France, Italy, Scandinavia, Japan, Latin America and elsewhere – was dependent on artisans.

Perriand's career is a fascinating case study within this larger phenomenon, for her embrace of craft techniques was unusually explicit, and also represented a forceful volte-face on her part – a repudiation of her own early ideas. In her 1929 manifesto 'Wood or Metal?', Perriand presented these two materials as exemplars of whole realms of production. After witheringly describing timber as 'a vegetable substance, in its very nature bound to decay', she noted acerbically that wood could never have been used to create the Eiffel Tower (which is true enough). Against this, she expressed a clear preference for industrialised production in metal: 'by means of the different means of manufacture it opens out new vistas; new opportunities of design ... METAL plays the same part in furniture as cement has done in architecture. IT IS A REVOLUTION.'[3]

Implicit in her words was a drive toward standardisation across all realms of design: conception, execution and use. This approach was, of course, consistent with that forcefully propounded at the time by her close associate Le Corbusier. Infamously, when first meeting Perriand in 1927 – she was then a young woman – he dismissed her with the remark, 'you know, we do not embroider cushions here', a comment chiefly remarkable for its blatant sexism, but also its disdain of conventional craft skills. And in 1929, in terms closely echoing Perriand's manifesto, he wrote with pride of their collaboration, in which 'the inventory of innumerable pieces of furniture passed down by tradition, and manufactured in wood in the Faubourg Saint-Antoine, is reduced to a few storage cabinets ... Metallic furniture is born.'[4]

By 1950, though, Le Corbusier was changing his tune. As Caroline Maniaque has explained, he engaged in an intensive collaboration with a group of Catalan masons for the construction of the Maisons Jaoul, whose most distinctive feature is their shallow vaulting in hand-laid brick.[5] And the famous V-leg chairs in teak (designed by Pierre Jeanneret and a team of Indian architects) that populated Le Corbusier's Chandigarh were also made, in huge numbers, by local craftspeople.[6]

Perriand was way ahead of him. Already in 1932, she wrote in an unpublished notebook:

> Work less in big factories, because the next stage in the evolution of machinery consists not in quantity but a change in human quality, slow down the pace of work, reduce nervous fatigue and change machinery that is harmful to people ... Man must not be modelled on the machine, but the machine on man.[7]

Over the following years, though she by no means turned her back on standardised solutions (she was fascinated by the possibility of prefabricated buildings, for example), Perriand began cultivating greater interest in raw materials, and closer working relationships with craftspeople. Just four years after her manifesto 'Wood or Metal?', she took a series of photographs showing freshly cut black locust logs, end-on: a Surrealistic 'found drawing', but also an emphatic celebration of the very material she had so recently maligned. In 1935, she created a Chaise à dossier basculant, based directly on a tubular-steel design she, Corbusier and Jeanneret had developed in 1928, but executed in carved wood with a rush seat. When she showed this chair at the Exposition Universelle in Brussels, other modernists (including the architect Pierre Chareau)

criticised it as retrograde – an abandonment of the true faith. Perriand, however, defended its artisan manufacture as simply an alternative form of efficiency: 'one can work honestly in any material, taking into account the context, means of production, and needs [compte tenu des lieux, des moyens de production, des besoins] ... It turned out that this chair could be manufactured for next to nothing by artisans without sophisticated machinery.'[8]

The key point Perriand makes here – that context matters, and decisions about both production and aesthetics should be made accordingly – may seem uncontroversial in retrospect. But it was precisely this concession that modernism, in its early absolutist form, had refused to make. This was a matter both of practicality and of principle: standardisation, with its promise of low cost and high quality, is incompatible with ad hoc variation; and the whole premise of design as a perfectible art, in which a form is honed to its purest and most exact expression, is necessarily threatened by the individual interpretation of the artisan. Yet by the mid-1930s, it was clear that these ideal principles were being observed mainly in the breach. If modernist objects were going to be made at all, they would probably have to be made by hand.

Perriand's willingness to adjust to diverse circumstance became vitally important when, in 1940, she went to Japan at the invitation of its Ministry of Commerce and Industry, to advise on design and export strategy. Politically, the moment was inauspicious. The Japanese entered into a pact with Nazi Germany, which had just invaded France, a month after her arrival. She carried on nonetheless, travelling the country with the young artist Sōri Yanagi. This was an intriguing connection, for he introduced Perriand to his father Sōetsu Yanagi, founder and lead theorist of the mingei movement, which venerated (some might say fetishised) vernacular objects as a remedy to the deadening effects of industrialism. The elder Yanagi knew very well that it was not possible for a modern designer to assume the identity of an 'unknown craftsman', but he did contend that anonymous historical objects were a vital source, in many respects superior to anything that could be mass-produced. Accordingly, he and his allies, including the potters Shōji Hamada and Kanjirō Kawai – whom Perriand met in Mashiko and Kyoto, respectively – sought to ground their own cosmopolitan sensibilities in the bracing reality of everyday rural life.

Thus, in Japan Perriand was presented not only with a culture quite alien to her own, but also an ideology exactly opposed to the one she had espoused only a decade earlier. In response to this global encounter, she demonstrated just how willing she was to allow 'context' to guide her actions. For her reaction was to embrace the *mingei* philosophy whole-heartedly, rejecting only the atmosphere of nostalgia that pervaded Sōetsu Yanagi's thought. After visiting the displays at his museum, the Mingeikan, she wrote in her notebook, 'What gives beauty and truth to these objects is that they serve. The people spontaneously created these objects in response to their needs.' Such precedents must not be statically replicated, she thought, but should instead serve as a jumping-off point for future development: 'The tradition must go forward. It must be better or it must be different ... how can I use them, use this splendid craft technique? Even as I breathe, the imagination is already at work.'[9]

In bamboo, Perriand found a material in which to apply these ideas. In September 1940, she visited a furniture company called Chikkosha, in Tokyo. Though its products were poor in quality, she was captivated by the inherent properties of the material they were using – strong and flexible and naturally abundant. Bamboo offered some of the tectonic qualities of tubular steel at a fraction of the expense. Perriand initiated an ambitious collaboration with Chikkosha, setting out to do for furniture something akin to what Hamada and Kawai had done for ceramics, infusing a traditional technique with a degree of self-conscious sophistication. Her forays in this direction again reprised the metal furniture she had designed with Jeanneret and Corbusier, including one design that retraced the lines of their famous B306 chaise longue, but set atop a massive *croix* (X-shaped) base. To upholster it, she employed woven rice-straw inspired by *mino*, the coats made by peasants in Tōhoku,

Bamboo and wood chaise longue, October 1940. Adaptation of the tubular *Chaise longue basculante* designed by Le Corbusier, Pierre Jeanneret, Charlotte Perriand, 1928

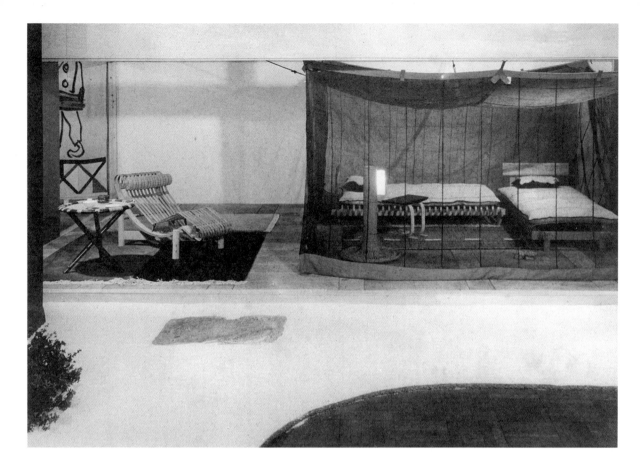

in northern Japan. It is a quintessential example of her hybridisation of past and present. As Charlotte Benton has written in a definitive study of her bamboo experiments, Perriand intended them to 'conserve folk memory and national or regional identity', while also 'rising to the challenge of developing forms and techniques for the volume production of new goods for external markets'.[10]

Perriand left Japan in November 1941 – only days before the attack on Pearl Harbor – but not before she had produced several objects in bamboo, woven wicker, lacquer and other materials, including an extraordinary table with a massive, natural-edge cherrywood top on an ironwork base, recalling her photographs of 1933, and also anticipating the later work of Japanese-American furniture maker George Nakashima.[11] In a curious echo of what had happened in Brussels, this application of Art Brut principles to furniture design

was forcefully criticised by Japanese observers, who clearly expected a different sort of modernism from their French visitor. Perriand also organised an exhibition for the Takashimaya department stores in Osaka and Tokyo, with the title *Contact with Japanese Art: Selection, Tradition, Creation*. In this vision of a syncretic reality yet to come, she presented her own prototypes and photographs, along with Japanese vernacular objects, a reproduction of a painting by her friend Fernand Léger, prints by Pablo Picasso, a carpet based on a sailor's doodle, and a large wall-hanging based on a child's drawing.

Selection, Tradition, Creation deserves to be much better known. A powerful demonstration of the possibilities of hand-made modernism, it was also one of the twentieth century's most prescient curatorial ventures, drawing on avant-garde modernism, *mingei* and Surrealism. Perriand anticipated

Relaxation area and bedroom in the exhibition *Contact with Japanese Art: Selection, Tradition, Creation*, Tokyo, 28 March to 6 April 1941

twenty-first-century methodologies that operate on her premise that 'assembling objects that contradict each other allows other forms of harmony to develop.'[12] In all these respects, it was a fitting capstone to Perriand's activities in Japan, which were brief in duration but strikingly far-sighted. Her Takashimaya shows anticipated, for example, the designer Clara Porset's 1952 *Art in Daily Life: An Exhibition of Well-Designed Objects Made in Mexico* (held at the Instituto Nacional de Bellas Artes in Mexico City), which similarly juxtaposed contemporary furnishings with vernacular source material, against a scenography of avant-garde photo-murals by Lola Álvarez Bravo. In Porset's project, as curator Zoë Ryan has written, 'the forces of tradition and modernity, craft and industry were not only reconciled, but promoted as a unique contribution to world culture.'[13]

Much the same could be said for Perriand's exhibition, as well as her collaboration with artisan producers like Chikkosha, which presaged other interventions in Japan. Perhaps the best-known example is Isamu Noguchi's *akari* lighting, which he began developing in

1951 after visiting Gifu at the invitation of the mayor there. Working in collaboration with Tameshiro Ozeki, head of a family lantern-making firm, he developed an ingenious extended series of lamps made of mulberry paper and thin bamboo strips. (The Ozeki workshop remained the sole producers of *akari* throughout Noguchi's lifetime.) The lights collapse down for ease of shipping, and, when unfolded, assume various abstract shapes. The runaway commercial success of Noguchi's series brought the opposite problem to the one that Perriand had faced before the war. He was obliged to defend their status as modern conceptions: 'if they didn't have that light bulb inside,' he liked to say, 'they'd have been treated as art all along.'[14]

In 1955, designer Russel Wright travelled to Japan under the auspices of the US government, as part of a broader tour of Asian nations. His brief – to consult on domestic production, in the hopes of spurring export trade – was not that different from Perriand's, though it took place against a very different political backdrop, as the US occupation of Japan had ended only three years previously.

Wright also arrived at a similar formula to Perriand, selecting exemplary vernacular crafts for development while also creating his own designs in ceramic and other media. As design historian Yuko Kikuchi notes, his visit coincided with the emergence of a novel Japanese term: *kurafuto*, a transliteration of the English word 'craft', denoting products that were made by artisans but serially produced (rather than one-offs), and meant to appeal to the contemporary lifestyle. Handmade modernism was gaining a global terminology.[15]

As for Perriand herself, she was still on the move. From Japan she first went to Hanoi, in what was then called Indochina, a French colonial possession. There she presented an exhibition of Japanese craft and then set about investigating the local traditions. This work was constantly interrupted by the war – she was obliged to leave in 1942 and spent a harrowing few months back in Japan trying to arrange passage back to France, but returned in 1943. Despite the brutal conflict raging all around her, she provided helpful guidance to textile, wood, lacquer, leather and paper artisans, presented exhibitions, and kept designing. Another chaise longue, on this occasion in rattan, was devised at this time to allow her to work while in a state of advanced pregnancy (her daughter Pernette was born in Hanoi in March 1944).[16]

Back in France after the war, Perriand signed an exclusive contract with Ateliers Jean Prouvé, joining forces with another modernist with a deep investment in craft. She was charged both with improving the aesthetic and practical aspects of existing standard models, and with developing new designs appropriate for serial production. Prouvé had begun his career as an ornamental blacksmith and, as the curator Christopher Wilk has noted, the imprint of that early experience remained on his work even as he scaled up to factory production: 'he knew intimately the processes of cutting, folding, and welding sheets of steel and of aluminium – reflected in the appearance of his designs.'[17] Of course,

the same was true of Perriand. Returning to the domain of metal fabrication – in this case, using folded sheet rather than tubes – she led on the design of a now-iconic range of case furniture for the dormitory rooms of Tunisian and Mexican students at the Cité universitaire in Paris. Though based on modular units, compatible with mass production, these were made in relatively short runs – just over a hundred, all told – and were prototyped by hand, under Perriand's direct supervision. This preparatory stage, too, was something that she considered in relation to craft traditions; as she later put it,

> model makers are at an impasse, whether working artisanally or in series. You might as well turn to pure craftsmanship, even if it appears to be a luxury ... At least we are saving these beautiful artisanal techniques which unfortunately tend to disappear and thereby become more and more expensive.[18]

A further significant stop on Perriand's global itinerary was Brazil, where she spent a great deal of time in the 1960s. Here again, she plunged headlong into an economy where craft was far more established than mass production, and considered how best to exploit the opportunity. In this case, she had a model to follow: Lina Bo Bardi, another European architect who had come to Brazil, in 1946. Arguing, somewhat counterintuitively, that her expatriate status made her representative of a national character compounded of many cultural traditions, Bo Bardi became an articulate exponent of the Brazilian vernacular. Her furniture designs took their overall lines from contemporaneous Italian modernism but reflected a local orientation in their materials (Brazilian woods, with leather and natural fibres for upholstery) and emphatically handmade character.[19]

Perriand first went to Brazil in 1959, to participate in a symposium in the newly built capital Brasília – a grand-scale application of Corbusian principles. While deeply impressed with its monumen-

Rio bookcase in Jacques Martin's apartment, Rio de Janeiro, 1963

tality, she believed that modernism in this country would inevitably have to shape itself in response to more local traditions: 'there is no one formula.'[20] When her husband Jacques Martin was named the head of Air France in Brazil, in 1962, she created an apartment in Rio de Janeiro incorporating all the key features of her handmade modernism: simply joined furniture, including a low table with a natural edge like the one she had exhibited in Japan, and locally sourced materials like jacaranda wood and rattan. The latter was used to particularly spectacular effect in a bookcase, following the composition of the pieces for Cité universitaire that she had produced with Prouvé but exploiting the weaving of the cane to create radially symmetrical patterns – an effect somewhat akin to book-matched veneer.

Viewed in isolation, Perriand's practice as a designer can seem idiosyncratic and anomalous. Present at the very inception of the International Style, and living an impressively cosmopolitan existence, she would have been in an ideal position to spread the faith of a single, repeatable, ideal model. Instead, she became a proponent of intelligent adaptation. And while always aware of the advantages of mass industry, she became a deep student of place-based craft idioms, incorporating them into her own work. Perriand was a unique figure, to be sure. But she was just one of many mid-century protagonists who placed great value on artisanship, seeing it not as inimical to avant-gardism, nor even as a preliminary phase, but as an infinitely variable, culturally expressive vocabulary in its own right. Setting her alongside figures like Sōetsu Yanagi, Russel Wright, Isamu Noguchi, Clara Porset and Lina Bo Bardi – a list that could be greatly extended – we can see that the incorporation of the hand-made into the story of modernism was no exception. It was the rule.

1   George Marcus, 'Disavowing Craft at the Bauhaus: Hiding the Hand to Suggest Machine Manufacture', *Journal of Modern Craft*, 1 (November 2008), 345–56.

2   Gökhan Karakuş, 'Handmade Modernity: Post-War Design in Turkey', in *Global Design History*, ed. Glenn Adamson, Giorgio Riello and Sarah Teasley (London: Routledge, 2011).

3   Charlotte Perriand, 'Wood or Metal?', *The Studio*, 97 (April 1929), 278–9.

4   Jacques Barsac, *Charlotte Perriand: Complete Works, Volume 1, 1903–1940* (Zurich: Scheidegger & Spiess, 2014), 146.

5   Caroline Maniaque, *Le Corbusier and the Maisons Jaoul* (Princeton, NJ: Princeton Architectural Press, 2009).

6   The story is well told by Avery Trufelman in her podcast on utopias: *Nice Try!*, episode 2: Chandigarh (June 2019).

7   Barsac (2014), 274.

8   Quoted on p.118 of Charlotte Benton, 'Le Corbusier: Furniture and the Interior', *Journal of Design History*, 3/2–3 (1990), 103–24.

9   Quoted in Jacques Barsac, *Charlotte Perriand: Complete Works, Volume 2, 1940–1955*, (Zurich: Scheidegger & Spiess, 2015), 25–6.

10   Quoted on p.45 of Charlotte Benton, 'From Tubular Steel to Bamboo: Charlotte Perriand, the Migrating *Chaise-longue* and Japan', *Journal of Design History*, 11/1 (1998), 31–58.

11   Barsac notes the similarity between the 1933 photographs and the slab table. See Barsac (2015), 68. On Nakashima, see George Nakashima, *The Soul of a Tree: A Master Woodworker's Reflections* (Tokyo: Kodansha, 1981).

12   Quoted in Barsac (2015), 86.

13   Zoë Ryan, *In a Cloud, In a Wall, In a Chair: Six Modernists in Mexico at Midcentury* (Chicago: Art Institute of Chicago and Yale University Press, 2019), 27.

14   Quoted in 'Isamu Noguchi: The Sculptor as Designer', *MoMA Magazine* 4 (Autumn 1977), 3.

15   See p.370 of Yuko Kikuchi, 'Russel Wright and Japan: Bridging *Japonisme* and Good Design through Craft', *Journal of Modern Craft*, 1 (November 2008), 357–82. See also Takuya Kida, 'Japanese Crafts and Cultural Exchange with the USA in the 1950s: Soft Power and John D. Rockefeller III during the Cold War', *Journal of Design History*, 25/4 (2012), 379–99.

16   See Barsac (2015), 128.

17   Marcus (2008).

18   Quoted in Pascal Renous, 'Charlotte Perriand', in *Portraits de Décorateurs* (Paris: Éditions H. Vial, Paris, 1969), 73–84. 'Actuellement ... les créateurs de modèles sont dans une impasse. Où bien on fait de l'artisanat, où bien dans la série ... Du moins sauvegarde-t-on ces belles technique artisanales qui tendent malheureusement à disparaître et deviennent par le fait même de plus en plus coûteuses.'

19   Aric Chen, *Brazil Modern: The Rediscovery of Twentieth-Century Brazilian Furniture* (New York: Monacelli Press, 2016), 119.

20   Jacques Barsac, *Charlotte Perriand: Complete Works, Volume 3, 1955–1968* (Zurich: Scheidegger & Spiess, 2017), 354.

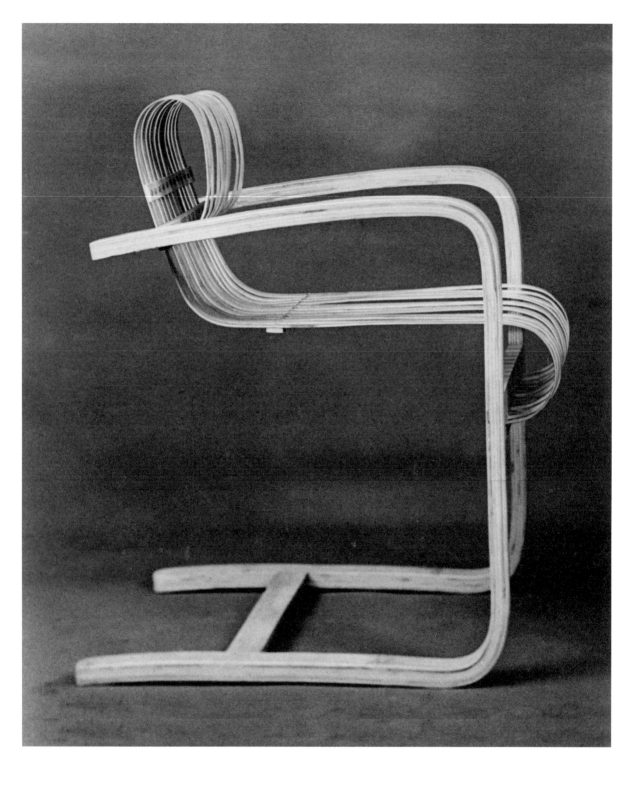

Cantilever bamboo chair, 1940

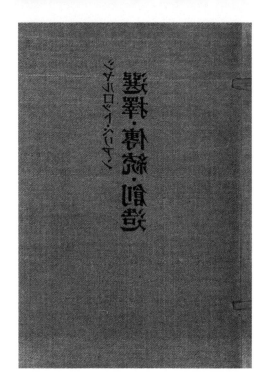

left   Charlotte Perriand in Japan, 1954
above   Charlotte Perriand, Junzō Sakakura, Exhibition catalogue for *Contact with Japanese Art: Selection, Tradition, Creation*, December 1941. Catalogue cover and plates 4, 5, and 25

In 1941, Perriand and architect Junzō Sakakura staged the exhibition *Contact with Japanese Art: Selection, Tradition, Creation* in the Takashimaya department store in Tokyo. At the beginning of the year, Perriand had been invited by the Japanese Ministry of Commerce, on Sakakura's recommendation, to offer practical advice to improve design for export crafts with the idea of increasing trade. Japan's economy was depressed and the government hoped to increase exports by producing modern Western-style products that drew on traditional Japanese crafts. The exhibition showcased Perriand's designs alongside objects from the Japan Folk Crafts Museum collection, set in traditional Japanese interiors. She included many of her early furniture designs, such as the cantilever chair and chaise longue, but now recreated in bamboo.

Interior in the exhibition *Contact with Japanese Art: Selection, Tradition, Creation*, Tokyo, 28 March–6 April 1941

Interior in the exhibition *Contact with Japanese Art: Selection, Tradition, Creation*, Osaka, 13–18 May 1941

Interiors in the exhibition *Contact with Japanese Art: Selection, Tradition, Creation*, Tokyo, 28 March–6 April 1941

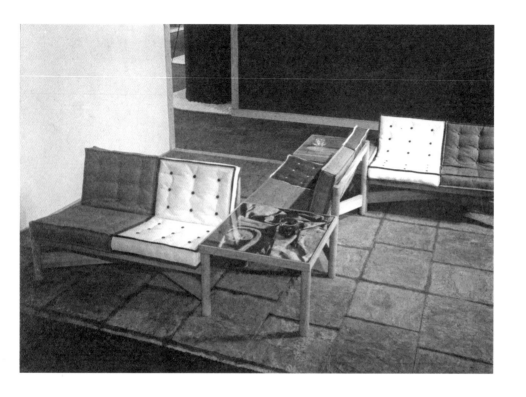

Interior in the exhibition *Contact with Japanese Art: Selection, Tradition, Creation*, Tokyo, 28 March–6 April 1941

Entrance to the exhibition *Contact with Japanese Art: Selection, Tradition, Creation*, Tokyo, 28 March–6 April 1941

Interior in the exhibition *Contact with Japanese Art: Selection, Tradition, Creation*, Osaka, 13–18 May 1941

Charlotte Perriand discusses her red pine table with cabinetmakers, 1940.
Jiro Hayashi in the foreground; on the left, Junzō Sakakura

above   Interior with sailor graffiti carpet in the exhibition *Contact with Japanese Art:*
Selection, Tradition, Creation, Tokyo, 28 March–6 April 1941

right   Sailor's chalk drawing on the deck of *Hakusan Maru*, 1940

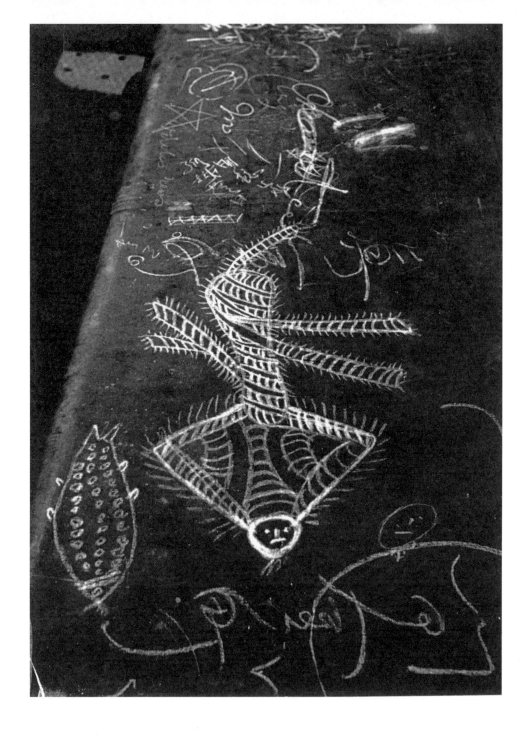

1   The design of this carpet was based on some chalk graffiti that Perriand photographed on the deck of the ship on which she sailed to Japan. It was the work of a Japanese sailor, but Perriand was so taken with it that she enlarged the image and transposed it directly onto the carpet.

above   Kitchen prototype for an apartment in Le Corbusier's Unité d'habitation, Marseille, 1949
right   Diagram of the kitchen–bar in Le Corbusier's Unité d'habitation, Marseille, 1949

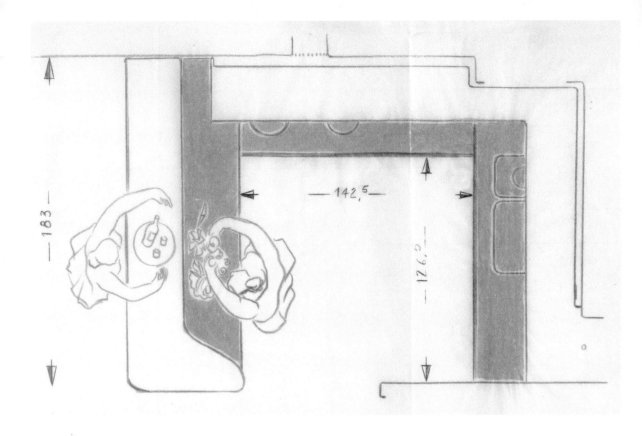

183

142,5

126,5

Le Corbusier invited Perriand to help him design the interiors of what would become his most famous housing project, the Unité d'habitation in Marseille. Perriand made a number of contributions, including the design of the kitchen, which was installed in 321 of the apartments. The layout created open-plan, flexible living spaces, with the kitchen–bar combined with the living room. Her design was based on ideas for a modern, labour-saving kitchen – developed by household reformers since the late nineteenth century. The kitchen was modular, featuring built-in cabinets with sliding doors and advanced features for the time: an electric stove with oven and fume hood, and a sink with integrated waste-disposal unit.

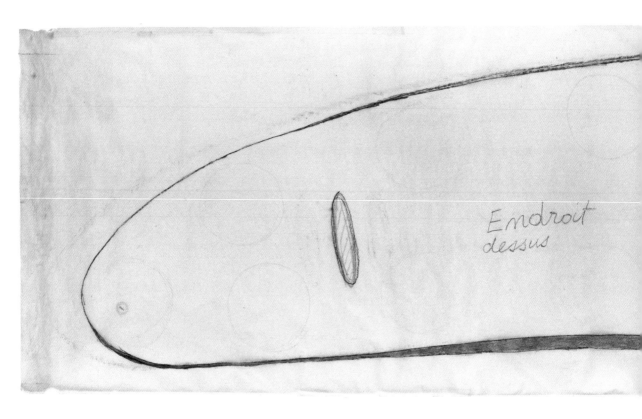

Template for the top of free-form dining table, August 1962. Also known as the Rio table

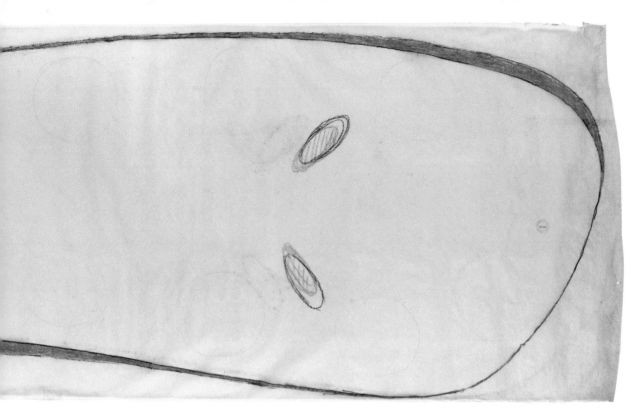

Free-form table, 1956

Perriand continued to develop her free-form table designs throughout her career. Although originally intended for her own use, some models, including this one, went into production through Galerie Steph Simon. This design includes spline joints to highlight its construction. The legs are placed close to the centre so seated guests avoid bumping them with their knees, while the table-top is shaped so that all those seated face the centre.

Jacques Martin's apartment, Rio de Janeiro, 1963

In 1961, Perriand's husband Jacques Martin was appointed general superintendent of Air France for Latin America and moved to an apartment in Rio de Janeiro. A year later, Perriand arrived to design the interiors. During a visit to a cabinetmaker, she was taken by an enormous piece of solid jacaranda wood. She chalked the surface with the outline for a table to seat fifteen people, with a top 6 centimetres (2.5 inches) thick and more than 4 metres (13 feet) long, taking the pattern of the grain into account. Reversing her usual working methods, she noted the dimensions to check against the size of the apartment.

Interior, *Proposal for a Synthesis of the Arts*, Takashimaya department store, Tokyo, 1955

In 1955, Perriand staged another exhibition in Tokyo, fourteen years after her first. Now a designer of international reputation, she used it to demonstrate some of the principles of what she called 'the art of dwelling'. The central idea was that art, architecture and industrial-manufacturing techniques should work in unison to create the modern home. This was what she called 'the synthesis of the arts'.

Entrance to the exhibition *Proposal for a Synthesis of the Arts*,
Takashimaya department store, Tokyo, 1955

Interiors, *Proposal for a Synthesis of the Arts*, Takashimaya department store, Tokyo, 1955

Double chaise longue, 1952

Double chaise longue, *Proposal for a Synthesis of the Arts*, Takashimaya department store, Tokyo, 1955.
Presented in the entrance to the exhibition

Charlotte Perriand at *Proposal for a Synthesis of the Arts*, Takashimaya department store, Tokyo, 1955

Interior, *Proposal for a Synthesis of the Arts*, Takashimaya department store, Tokyo, 1955

Woman posing on a stackable low lounge chair, referred to as 'the Conversation chair',
Proposal for a Synthesis of the Arts, Takashimaya department store, Tokyo, 1955

Tripod stool, 1946

Perriand designed various versions of this three-legged stool – all loosely modelled on the shepherd's stools
she saw in the mountainous Savoie region of France, where she liked to walk and ski. She admired the economy
of means by which shepherds could make themselves comfortable. This particular stool was designed for her
husband's business residence in Tokyo.

above   *Ombre* (Shadow) stacking chair, 1954
This stacking chair was made from a single sheet of plywood, cut and bent into shape. Perriand called
it *Ombre* after the Japanese shadow theatre, because it cuts a shadowy silhouette.

below   Air France stacking table, 1954
Perriand was interested in the Japanese tradition of using individual folding tables that could be stacked
after mealtimes, rather than seating everyone at a single large table. Her version is designed from a single
sheet of aluminium, folded like a piece of origami. It was produced by Jean Prouvé's workshop and was
named Air France after the company for which her husband worked as an executive.

Fernand Léger, *Sans titre: l'enfant à l'oiseau* (Untitled: child with a bird), ceramic, 1953

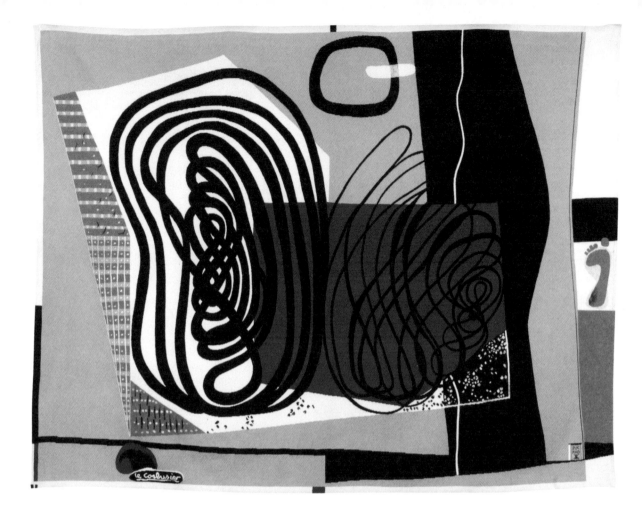

Le Corbusier, *Les huit* (The eight) tapestry, 1963

Isamu Noguchi, light fixtures, Galerie Steph Simon, Paris, c.1957

Isamu Noguchi, light fixtures, Galerie Steph Simon, Paris, c.1960
Charlotte Perriand, Dining table, free-form cabinet, *Nuage* (Cloud) bookcase
Verner Panton, Bachelor chair

Nuage (Cloud) bookshelf, Galerie Steph Simon edition, c. 1958

Since her first visit to Japan in 1940, Perriand had been struck by the shelving units she saw at Kyoto's Katsura Imperial Villa. '[They were] arranged on the walls, in the form of a cloud,' she wrote in her journal. Nearly a decade later, she unveiled *Nuage* (Cloud), a modular bookshelf of standardised parts that could be rearranged in various configurations, and includes sliding panels, trays and shelves. It was produced and sold by Steph Simon and gained popularity in the 1950s and 1960s.

modular designs for modern living

sébastian cherruet
jane hall

sébastain cherruet

beyond design

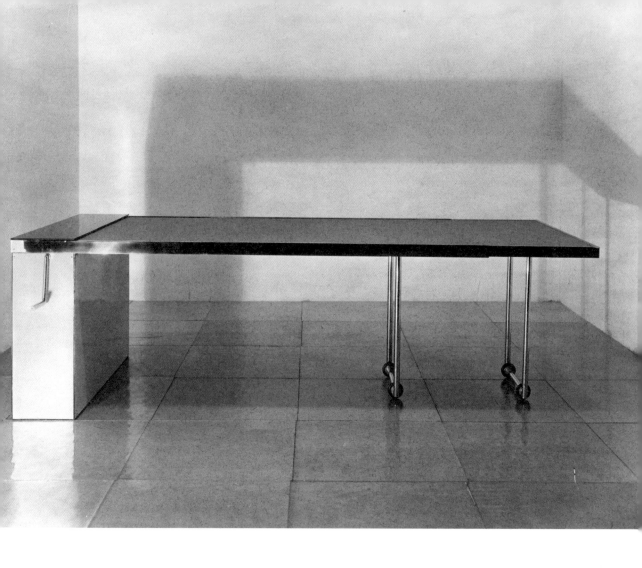

previous Bookcase for student's room, Maison du Mexique, 1952
above *Table extensible à manivelle* (Extendable table with crank mechanism), 1930

Although Charlotte Perriand did not define herself as a designer, from the 1920s onwards she created modern furniture classics that can now be found in some of the world's most prestigious museums. But Perriand did not envision her designs as individual objects detached from their context and conditions of production – for her, architecture encompassed not only the unchangeable aspects of a space but also its furnishings. Together they formed a whole whose essential qualities were to be found in the voids between the constituent parts. In other words, Perriand was designing the space between things as much as the things themselves. This attitude was exemplified in the modular storage systems that she designed, which invited each inhabitant to model their own space according to their specific needs. In this matrix uniting design and architecture, a new 'art of living' in tune with the times could come into being.

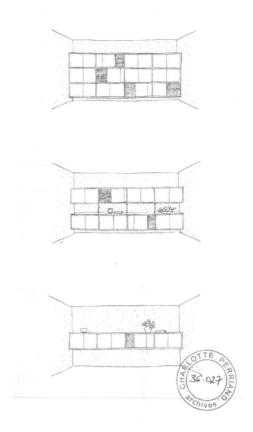

pioneer of modernity

In 1926, just after graduating from the school of the Union centrale des arts décoratifs, Perriand exhibited her *Coin de salon* (Sitting-room corner) at the Salon des artistes décorateurs. Realised in the Art Deco style of her first mentors, Maurice Dufresne and Henri Rapin, it comprised a luxuriously veneered desk, an armchair with a faceted back and a table whose elegance was praised by the magazine *Vogue*.[1] When, a year later, she exhibited her astonishing *Bar sous le toit* (Bar under the roof) at the 1927 Salon d'Automne, wood had suddenly given way to the chromed metal of the gleaming automobiles that Perriand so admired on the Champs-Élysées.[2] This stylistic evolution was first and foremost the result of a new approach: breaking with the *ensembliers décorateurs*, who generally offered catalogues of solid-wood furniture designed for bourgeois interiors, Perriand proposed a piece of integrated interior design, her *Bar sous le toit* having been conceived for a corner of the apartment–atelier she had recently moved into with her first husband, Percy Scholefield.

With its gaming table and phonograph, this home bar was modern not only in its forms but also in its programme – a liberated woman, Perriand kept her maiden name and had every intention of taking part in the Roaring Twenties, a time of partying and emancipation. Essentially unknown beforehand, she achieved a certain fame with her bar, which was widely covered in the trade press, both French and foreign. A *New York Times* article on 'diminutive bars, to be installed in the homes of American gentlemen in Paris' (a round-up of those shown at the Salon d'Automne) noted that, 'Of them all, the "bar sous le toit" designed by Charlotte Perriand is the most desirable.'[3] A few months later, at the Salon des artistes décorateurs in the Grand Palais, Perriand exhibited a modern dining room – alongside a smoking room by René Herbst and a living room by Djo-Bourgeois – displaying her extendable table and pivoting chair in a space that mimicked the volumes of her Place Saint-Sulpice apartment. At barely twenty-four, she appeared as one

'La ménagère et son foyer. Conseils pratiques sur l'équipement du logis' (The Homemaker and Her Home: Practical Advice for Equipping a Dwelling), *La femme et la vie*, no. 26 (1 May 1936)

of the figures of the avant-garde alongside the greatest designers of her times. Though initially conceived for the restricted space of her atelier, the pieces were intended to be mass-produced, as demonstrated by the patent she took out for the table and Thonet's production of her pivoting chair.

Perriand's talent earned her the esteem of Le Corbusier, for whom she began working at the end of 1927. The challenge was two-fold: on the one hand, learning new skills as an architect and, on the other, contributing to the development of a series of modern furnishings. For while Le Corbusier was promoting the five points of his doctrine in 1927 in *L'Esprit nouveau*, the furniture he used in his projects earned him the mockery of his German confrères: compared with the astonishing cantilever of Mies van der Rohe's tubular-steel chairs, Le Corbusier – in his 1925 Pavillon de l'Esprit nouveau – could only propose a nineteenth-century bentwood chair produced by Michael Thonet. During her time at the rue de Sèvres office, Perriand designed some of the icons of modernity: the tubular-steel chaise longue, the *Grand confort* armchair and a table with aeroplane-wing legs, all of which were shown at the 1929 Salon d'Automne. Though her role with respect to these pieces was long eclipsed by Le Corbusier, who published his *Oeuvre complète* during his lifetime, she was nonetheless a designer who had already achieved critical recognition and who participated fully in the adventure of the 1920s avant-garde.

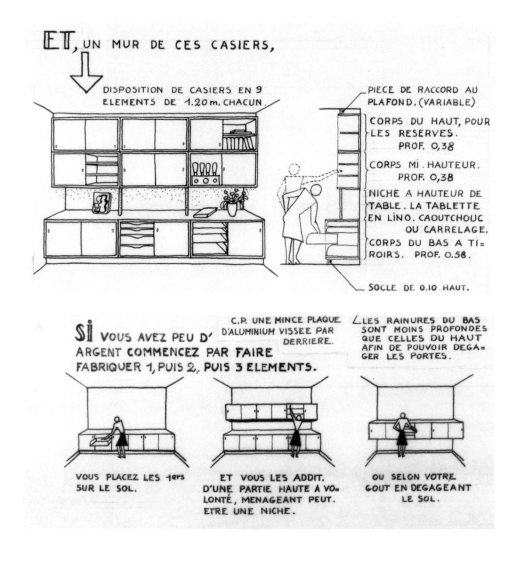

'La ménagère et son foyer. Conseils pratiques sur l'équipement du logis', *La femme et la vie*, no. 26 (1 May 1936)

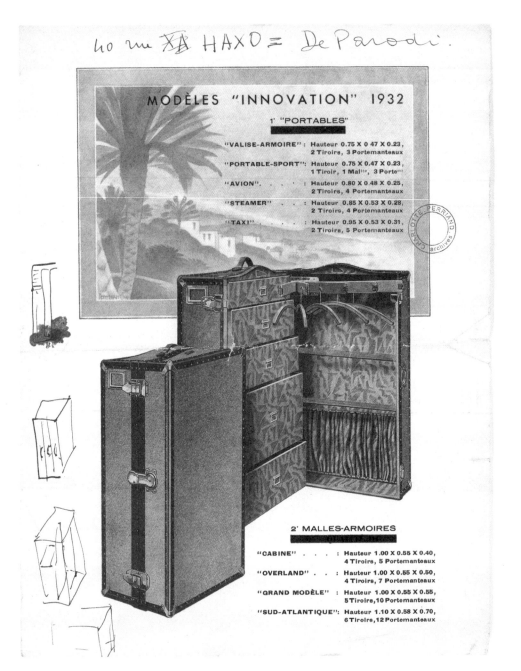

40 rue XB HAXO = De Parodi.

MODÈLES "INNOVATION" 1932

1' "PORTABLES"

"VALISE-ARMOIRE" :	Hauteur 0.75 X 0 47 X 0.23, 2 Tiroirs, 3 Portemanteaux
"PORTABLE-SPORT" :	Hauteur 0.75 X 0.47 X 0.23, 1 Tiroir, 1 Mal^(lle), 3 Porte^(ux)
"AVION" . . . :	Hauteur 0.80 X 0.48 X 0.25, 2 Tiroirs, 4 Portemanteaux
"STEAMER" . . :	Hauteur 0.85 X 0.53 X 0.28, 2 Tiroirs, 4 Portemanteaux
"TAXI" . . . . :	Hauteur 0.95 X 0.53 X 0.31, 2 Tiroirs, 5 Portemanteaux

2' MALLES-ARMOIRES

"CABINE" . . . :	Hauteur 1.00 X 0.55 X 0.40, 4 Tiroirs, 5 Portemanteaux
"OVERLAND" . . :	Hauteur 1.00 X 0.55 X 0.50, 4 Tiroirs, 7 Portemanteaux
"GRAND MODÈLE" :	Hauteur 1.00 X 0.55 X 0.55, 5 Tiroirs, 10 Portemanteaux
"SUD-ATLANTIQUE":	Hauteur 1.10 X 0.58 X 0.70, 6 Tiroirs, 12 Portemanteaux

Innovation trunk, published in *L'Esprit nouveau*, no. 27 (1924)

Perriand's strength lay in her ability to remain in tune with her times. In her 1929 manifesto 'Wood or Metal?', published in the magazine *The Studio*, she proclaimed the advantages of metal, which she saw as the key to a revolution in furniture as fundamental as that produced by reinforced concrete in architecture. Metal was the material for a 'new man ... the type of individual who keeps pace with scientific thought, who understands his age and lives with it: the aeroplane, the ocean liner and the motor are at his service'.[5] Yet, from the 1930s, Perriand once again started to use wood for her furniture. In the *Maison du jeune homme* (House for a young man), shown at Brussels in 1935, she displayed, opposite a chromed armchair that pivoted on ball bearings, a chair in wood and straw. The opposition between the two surprised her contemporaries, such as Pierre Chareau, who accused her of 'betraying the moderns'.[6] Besides the form, it was first and foremost the manner of production that differed: on the one hand industrial manufacture, on the other the vernacular know-how of a craftsman-carpenter. In the 1920s, the machine was still synonymous with freedom from manual work, but after the 1929 Crash and the Depression that followed, the omnipotence of the machinist model was called into question – where once it had seemed the promise of progress, it now appeared a tool of capitalism and the rush to re-arm. Perriand's interest in the conditions of production – today we would say in their environmental and societal impact – is essential to her work. Her wooden stools evoke the Savoyard shepherds who used them, as well as local craft know-how. Before designing a piece of furniture, Perriand considered the available techniques and materials, which needed to be understood before being put to use. Her magnificent forms are never gratuitous.

In the 1930s, photographs of Art Brut began to appear in Perriand's oeuvre, among them shots of compressed sheet metal that demonstrate a critical approach at odds with the enthusiasm inherent in the machinist style

of her early pieces. Where, in 1928, she lit her Place Saint-Sulpice dining room with a car headlight, fixed to the wall like a readymade, in the early 1930s she turned her gaze towards the creations of nature more than those of industry. In the forests outside Paris and on the beaches of Normandy, she collected gorgeous rough stones, driftwood and ephemeral blocks of ice whose transparency delighted her. Perriand displayed these objects of 'poetic reaction' in the manner of a Confucian scholar seeking his philosophy in the beauty of natural forms. At the 1937 Exposition Internationale in Paris, Perriand showed new furniture in the Union des artistes modernes pavilion, a group of which she was a founding member. While her tubular-steel armchair echoed the glass-and-steel building designed by her modernist colleagues, she also exhibited wooden armchairs and tables whose tops were printed with blown-up photographs – Art Brut was integrated into the design.

The following year, as she was moving into a new atelier in the Montparnasse neighbourhood, Perriand designed a 'free-form' table: made by an artisan, it stood out due to its asymmetrical form and the thick curve of its top, inviting not only the eye but also the hand to partake of its sensuality. This phenomenological approach implied both caressing the object and moving within the fluid space around it, for what Perriand had designed was perhaps less a table-sculpture than the volume of air around it. At first glance, the functionalist approach underpinning her 1928 extendable table seems to have been abandoned here; but do humans actually walk about orthogonally, like robots turning sharply at right angles? In this sense, the free-form table is highly functional, its curves both offering a hollow in which to sit and facilitating movement through the room. In the work of many architects and designers of a modernist bent, the commitment to functionalism and structural rationalism was no doubt rhetorical. For, in reality, Perriand's 1928 pivoting chair was costly to produce and no lighter than a straw chair – which is, moreover, easier to repair. The modernity of tubular-steel furniture was more symbolic than practical. While certain modernist architects considered timber heretical, Perriand's designs in wood – easy to repair, environmentally friendly, imbued with the intelligence of the hand – now appear thoroughly modern. Are her wooden tables less modern than her tubular-steel furniture? For Perriand, tradition was synonymous with innovation, the use of vernacular craft never being a question of backward-looking forms. During her time in Japan, she advocated the use of vernacular techniques that would allow new forms to be born without imitating European production. This was the purpose of her 1941 Tokyo exhibition, which shone a spotlight on bamboo, a material she used to rethink her famous chaise longue and also for new pieces: the shadows they cast were as much a part of the design as the solid matter itself. But Perriand never set industry against craft: throughout her entire career, from the 1920s to the end of the century, her designs were the result of a pragmatic approach that refused all dogmatism. At Les Arcs ski resort in Savoie, she included both prefabricated fibreglass bathroom units and furniture crafted in wood. A few months before she died, in 1999, she was talking about exploring the potential of carbon fibre and soft plastics, which she had discovered in the latest bicycle saddles. By calling on both craft and industry, her intention was to create objects that were modern, sustainable and adapted to humans.

from design pieces to furniture systems: a dialogue between form and use

With her experiments in modularity, Perriand made yet another contribution to the history of design. In her autobiography, *Une vie de création*, she described her parents' apartment, full of mismatching knick-knacks that she wished would just disappear – 'Luckily we had a cat who regularly knocked them over'[7] – as well as the soothing calm of her empty hospital room after an appendicitis operation. These childhood memories illustrate Perriand's lifelong quest to free domestic space from the superfluous. While working at Le Corbusier's office, she became friends with Junzō Sakakura, who gave her Kakuzō Okakura's *The Book of Tea*, which includes Laozi's maxim: 'Vacuum is all potent because all containing.'[8] From the 1920s to the 1990s, Perriand imagined furniture systems designed to free up space. Where the 1929 Salon d'Automne is concerned, history has chosen to remember the iconic tubular-steel furniture, of which the adjustable chaise longue was no doubt the most emblematic. But the most radical project was perhaps the metal storage system, which formed an astonishing partition of cupboards that was as much a part of the architecture as of the furniture. This standardised storage unit played several roles in the Salon display: a separation between the bedrooms and living rooms, a low piece of furniture beneath the Corbusian horizontal window and a partition with a serving hatch separating the kitchen from the dining room. The basic structure was made from square tubes, with a rectangular frame that could be added so as to combine two cubes, which could themselves be separated by metal sheets and closed thanks to sliding doors in glass or polished or lacquered metal. Designed by Perriand, Le Corbusier and Pierre Jeanneret, the system allowed infinite permutations by juxtaposing or superimposing the basic modules, which could be filled either with shelves or drawers thanks to integrated supports that doubled up as runners.

Sketch of the *Nuage* (Cloud) bookcase with side panels, record player compartment, record shelves, built-in radio and bar, 1956

Though these storage units did not sell as well as was hoped – but then neither did the tubular-steel furniture, which was produced by Thonet in only very small quantities – the system anticipated by a quarter of a century that proposed in 1956 by the French designers Pierre Guariche, Joseph-André Motte and Michel Mortier, working together under the moniker ARP, and produced by Minvielle. For the brand USM, Paul Schärer and Fritz Haller brought the system up to date in the 1960s through the use of an ingenious connecting ball.

It was no longer a question of designing a furniture-object associated with a style, but rather of offering a system that could be adapted in both time and space according to need. This new approach to furnishing involved not only the designer but also the user, for it is the latter who decides the combination of modules that will fit the situation. In 1936, in the weekly paper *Vendredi*, Perriand published an illustrated article about the furnishing of the home in which she condemned the outdated styles and poor ergonomics of traditional furniture. 'Go take the pile of plates from behind the pile of cups!' On the basis of a Taylorist analysis of movement, she imagined a wall storage unit whose drawers and shallow depth would make the entirety of its volume easily accessible. In her archives, there are advertisements for Innovation steamer trunks, whose rationality allowed space to be optimised. The challenge was no longer to create an ornament at the scale of the dwelling but to satisfy a need, an approach that broke with the classic bourgeois interior, where the erratic volumes of chests of drawers, sideboards, bookshelves and other massive pieces of furniture clogged up the space. Aware that there was not yet an industrial producer of the *Vendredi* storage unit, she included plans so that each household could have its own made by a carpenter. 'If you don't have a lot of money, start by making 1 then 2 then 3 parts,' she wrote.

The post-war commission to fit out student rooms at Paris's Cité universitaire internationale allowed Perriand to continue her experiments

Large storage unit with side panels and polyester sliding doors, 1965. Issued by Galerie Steph Simon, 1965

with wall storage. For the Maison du Mexique (1952), she designed a bookshelf that served to divide the sleeping space from the washbasin. Placed on top of tiled masonry supports, it could not be moved, but the varying rhythm of shelf heights, as well as the vertical pieces in bent sheet metal finished in different colours, helped break the monotony often characteristic of prefabrication. For the Maison de la Tunisie (also 1952), Perriand designed a bookshelf placed against the wall whose lower shelf was prolonged in space all the way to the window. To enrich her designs, she called on the talents of others: Jean Prouvé, whose workshops produced the bent-steel supports, and three artists for the colour schemes – Sonia Delaunay, Nicolas Schöffer and Silvano Bozzolini. Rather than proposing monofunctional models that served either as simple partitions or shelving, she demonstrated a plasticity in her designs and – from one student hall to another, thanks to the polychromy – was able to introduce a diversity that was nonetheless compatible with the requirements of mass production. Perriand also envisaged commercialising these designs – whose origins can be traced back to the 1929 storage units – in the form of a series of prefabricated pieces that each household could combine to suit its needs. To do this, she began working on the standardisation of the different parts, such as moulded-plastic drawers that could be used in different pieces of furniture following the prototype shown in the 1955 Tokyo exhibition *Proposal for a Synthesis of the Arts*. For this synthesis, in which the fine and decorative arts find harmony, was only possible in a space freed up, thanks to the standardisation of stackable chairs and rational storage units, from the background noise too often generated by disparate furniture cluttered with baubles and knick-knacks.

The modular and participatory design advocated by Perriand involved a certain modesty on her part, in the sense that she was no longer the sole author of a piece of sculpture–furniture but the instigator of a system whose multiple permutations she did not entirely control. In this respect, it is interesting to note the paradoxical reception that greeted her *Nuage* (Cloud) bookshelves, which the Galerie Steph Simon began selling in the 1950s. Following the principles set forth in *Vendredi*, Perriand designed what was first and foremost a storage system – the combination of metal supports, shelves, sliding doors and drawers allowing for infinite permutations, as vaunted in the sales brochure *Bibliothèques à plots Charlotte Perriand*, which underlined these 'possibilities of variation of arrangement'. Given that this novel approach to design was launched in the context of a market used only to fixed-form furniture, Steph Simon asked Perriand to put together a few model variations to give examples of how the pieces might be combined. The visual balance between the orthogonal grid and the dynamism of the asymmetrical compositions she suggested was an immediate hit, whose beauty is still appreciated today. These display combinations can now be found in museums, set up on podiums and entirely empty, exhibited as sculpture rather than a storage system. Stripped of their function and presented as though they were unique pieces, these fixed combinations are the antithesis of the open system, adaptable to use and context, that Perriand imagined.

towards a modular architecture

Conscious of her strength as a furniture designer, Perriand knocked on Le Corbusier's door with a desire to become an architect, a profession of which she was largely ignorant in 1927. It was while working with the master of modernism that she imagined a coherence between design, architecture and urbanism through the use of modules. Though his *modulor* would not be fully codified until after the war, Le Corbusier was already using proportional systems – 'regulating lines', as he called them – in the 1920s to ensure unity between the different parts of his buildings. In Le Corbusier's office, as of 1929, Perriand began studies for a 14-square-metre (150-square-foot) cell, a minimal 'biological element' for the dwelling. For Perriand, emptiness was a precious material; where the classic bourgeois apartment consisted of rooms with specific fixed functions, she designed sliding partitions that allowed different spaces to be united, meaning the home could enjoy maximum space in the daytime. These principles would inform, decades later, the design of Le Corbusier's Unités d'habitation. In tandem with her interest in the vernacular architecture of the Alps and the shores of the Mediterranean, Perriand took part in the Congrès internationaux d'architecture moderne (CIAM), which advocated large-scale standardisation and prefabrication. Published in 1935 in *L'Architecture d'aujourd'hui*, her *Maison au bord de l'eau* (House by the water) was the result of her personal research into such ideas, in which she mixed a poetics of living with industrialisation of the dwelling.[9] With respect to her *Tritrianon* project (1937), made up of juxtaposed cells, she explained that she had taken the width of a bed as a basic dimension, 'the largest dimension useful to man'.[10] Even before her sojourn in Japan, she designed modular free plans with sliding partitions whose volumes opened generously on to the exterior. Her Japanese adventure would prove to be less a discovery than a validation of her preoccupations: her observation of housing in Tokyo confirmed for her that a standardised model is possible at a large scale while still offering remarkable diversity.

Perriand's ideas were not simply pipe dreams. With the engineer André Tournon, she designed a prefabricated mountain refuge, which was shown in 1937 on the banks of the Seine in Paris before being assembled at Saint-Nicolas de Véroce in the Alps. The following year, with Pierre Jeanneret, she designed a more ambitious model, the Refuge Tonneau, as well as working on plans for a hotel, part of whose exterior was to be planted so that it would dissolve into the landscape. These principles would come into play in the 1960s at Les Arcs ski resort, a high-altitude holiday town in which she pursued her approach of designing from the smallest domestic object up to the largest at an urban scale.

She imagined generous light-filled rooms where one could lunch with a view of the Alpine peaks, before, at nightfall, converting the banquettes for sleeping and collapsing the tables to bedside height. Rather than transporting to the mountainside the irrational and compartmentalised bourgeois apartment, with its bedrooms, kitchens, dining rooms and so on, she proposed a modular multifunctional plan that helped reduce the volume of her buildings, whose roofline followed the valley's slope out of respect for the landscape she so adored.

'Friend, do not enter without desire,' wrote the poet Paul Valéry. While Perriand's work constitutes a window on to the history of twentieth-century art, it is possible to see more there than just a legacy from the past. Hers is an oeuvre that questions humanity's place with respect to industry and nature, her modular design inviting us to become co-authors of a new 'art of living' that respects diversity and is conscious of our impact on the environment.

1   Jean Gallotti, 'Les petites tables ou fortunes des guéridons', *Vogue* (1 February 1927), 41.
2   Charlotte Perriand, *Une vie de création* (Paris: Odile Jacob, 1998), 23.
3   'Bars and Interiors Shown at the Salon', *New York Times* (December 1927). Press cutting held in the Archives Charlotte Perriand.
4   This subtitle was inspired by the title of Gaston Bachelard's 1957 book *La poétique de l'espace*, in which he theorises a phenomenology of architecture.
5   Charlotte Perriand, 'Wood or Metal?', *The Studio*, 97 (January 1929), 49–50.
6   Jacques Barsac, *Charlotte Perriand, l'œuvre complète, 1903–1914* (Paris: Norma, 2015), 342.
7   Perriand (1998), 430.
8   Kakuzō Okakura, *The Book of Tea*, http://pdf-objects.com/files/Book-Of-Tea.pdf [1 April 2021]
9   'Concours pour une maison de week-end', *L'Architecture d'aujourd'hui*, 1 (January 1935), 13.
10 This is the first of the *7 points constructifs* ('seven points of construction') set down by Perriand. See Barsac (2015), 327.

Bookcase for student's room, Maison du Mexique, 1952

In 1952, Perriand was commissioned to design the interiors of the Maison du Mexique, a dormitory for Mexican students on the outskirts of Paris. There were seventy-seven rooms to fit out. Her first move was to replace the partition wall between the bedroom and bathroom with one of her bookcases. Acting as both room divider and storage unit, it made the rooms feel bigger.

Charlotte Perriand, Silvano Bozzolini, Nicolas Schöffer, Sonia Delaunay, Colour variations of the bookshelf for Maison de la Tunisie, 1/10 scale models, 1952

At the same time as fitting out the interiors of the Maison du Mexique, Perriand was doing the same for the Maison de la Tunisie, which housed Tunisian students. Here she opted for a different approach, placing a storage unit integrated with a long bench along one wall of each bedroom. A number of artists were assigned to create the colour schemes for the rooms such as Sonia Delaunay, Silvano Bozzolini, Nicolas Schöffer and Perriand herself.

above   Room in the Maison de la Tunisie of the Cité universitaire internationale, Paris, 1952
right   Jean Prouvé and Charlotte Perriand, c.1953

Modular furniture was gaining popularity in post-war Europe and the United States. Made of standardised parts that were industrially produced, such furniture was affordable and adaptable. In Perriand's work, this concept was realised through her collaboration with the engineer and designer Jean Prouvé. Prouvé hired Perriand to design furniture that his workshop could make and sell. The most famous outcome of this partnership was her *bibliothèques* (bookcases).

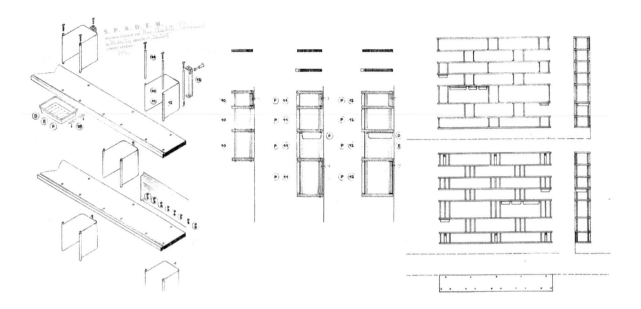

Elevations, plans, cross sections and axonometric drawings of the standardised
mounting system for the Tunisie-type bookcases, June 1954

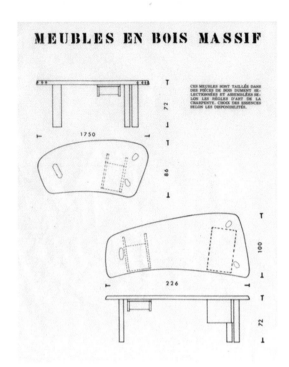

MEUBLES EN BOIS MASSIF

CES MEUBLES SONT TAILLÉS DANS DES PIÈCES DE BOIS DUMENT SELECTIONNÉES ET ASSEMBLÉES SELON LES RÈGLES D'ART DE LA CHARPENTE. CHOIX DES ESSENCES SELON LES DISPONIBILITÉES.

72
1750
86
100
226
72

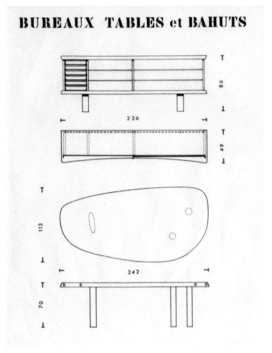

BUREAUX TABLES et BAHUTS

86
226
49
113
242
70

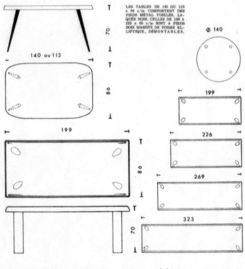

CHARLOTTE PERRIAND

LES TABLES DE 140 OU 113 x 86 c/m COMPORTENT DES PIEDS MÉTAL FUSELÉS, LAQUÉS NOIR. CELLES DE 199 à 323 x 86 c/m SONT A PIEDS BOIS MASSIFS DE FORME ELLIPTIQUE, DÉMONTABLES.

70
140 ou 113
86
199
86
70

Ø 140
199
226
269
323

EDITIONS STEPH SIMON   145, boulevard st.germain
paris 6eme   ODE 74.75

Drawings for solid-wood furniture, desks, tables and sideboards, 1956.
Galerie Steph Simon brochure

RANGEMENTS CHARLOTTE

ÉLÉMENTS DE RANGEMENT CONSTITUÉS PAR ASSEMBLAGE DE JOUES ET FONDS MÉTALLIQUES
LAQUÉS NOIR , ENTRETOISANT DES PLATEAUX EN LATTÉ PLAQUÉ FRÊNE OU MERISIER.

BLOC 3 B + 377 + BLOC 5 C

ASSEMBLAGE DE 2 BLOCS 3 B ET 2 BLOCS 5 C.

LES QUATRE TYPES DE BLOCS
CORRESPONDENT A DEUX FOR-
MATS DES TIROIRS CHARLOTTE
PERRIAND TYPE B ET C .
LEUR AMÉNAGEMENT PEUT ÉGA-
LEMENT COMPORTER DES RAYON-
NAGES EN GLACE OU EN BOIS.

BLOC 5 B + 566 + BLOC 8 C

+ 598 +   + 363 +

LES BLOCS PEUVENT ÊTRE JUXTAPOSÉS
OU SUPERPOSÉS POUR CONSTITUER DES
ENSEMBLES MEUBLES.

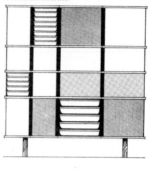

ASSEMBLAGE DE 4 BLOCS. 5 B ET 2 BLOCS 8 C.

+ 46 +

LA NORMALISATION DE CES DIF-
FÉRENTS ÉLÉMENTS PERMET DE
NOMBREUSES UTILISATIONS :
- RANGEMENTS DIVERS - GRAND
LINGE - LINGE DE CORPS - LIN-
GERIE - VAISSELLE - ARGENTERIE
- VERRERIE,
- BIBLIOTHÈQUE - RADIO - BAR
TOURNE-DISQUE - CLASSEMENT
DE DISQUES - DISPOSITION DE
DOSSIERS SUSPENDUS.
LES TIROIRS ÉQUIPANT CES MEU-
BLES DE RANGEMENT SONT RÉA-
LISÉS EN POLYSTYRÈNE DE QUA-
TRE COULEURS : ROUGE, JAUNE,
NOIR ET GRIS CLAIR.
LES PORTES COULISSANTES EXÉ-
CUTÉES EN POLYESTER AUX CINQ
COULEURS: ROUGE , JAUNE, NOIR ,
GRIS ET BLANC - POSSIBILITÉ DE
PORTES EN GLACE.

DÉPOSÉS BREVETÉS

MODÈLES TIROIRS

P E R R I A N D

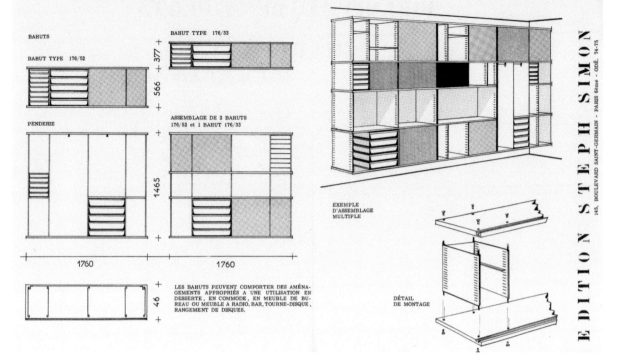

BAHUTS

BAHUT TYPE 176/52

BAHUT TYPE 176/33

PENDERIE

ASSEMBLAGE DE 2 BAHUTS
176/52 et 1 BAHUT 176/33

377

566

1465

46

1760

1760

EXEMPLE
D'ASSEMBLAGE
MULTIPLE

DÉTAIL
DE MONTAGE

LES BAHUTS PEUVENT COMPORTER DES AMÉNA-
GEMENTS APPROPRIÉS A UNE UTILISATION EN
DESSERTE, EN COMMODE, EN MEUBLE DE BU-
REAU OU MEUBLE A RADIO, BAR, TOURNE-DISQUE,
RANGEMENT DE DISQUES.

EDITION STEPH SIMON

145, BOULEVARD SAINT-GERMAIN - PARIS 6ème - ODÉ. 74-75

BIBLIOTHEQUE A PLOTS

CHARLOTTE PERRIAND

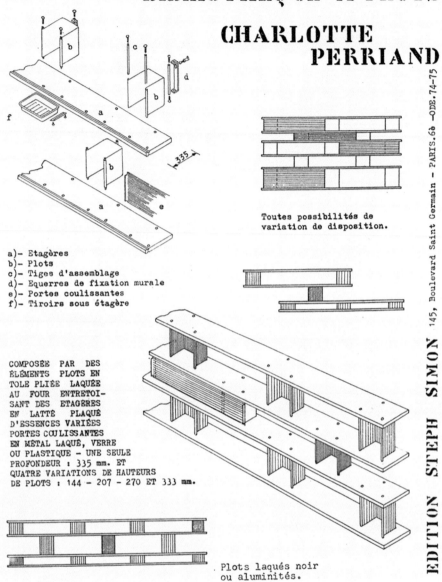

Toutes possibilités de variation de disposition.

a)- Etagères
b)- Plots
c)- Tiges d'assemblage
d)- Equerres de fixation murale
e)- Portes coulissantes
f)- Tiroirs sous étagère

COMPOSÉE PAR DES ÉLÉMENTS PLOTS EN TOLE PLIÉE LAQUÉE AU FOUR ENTRETOISANT DES ETAGÈRES EN LATTÉ PLAQUÉ D'ESSENCES VARIÉES PORTES COULISSANTES EN MÉTAL LAQUÉ, VERRE OU PLASTIQUE – UNE SEULE PROFONDEUR : 335 mm. ET QUATRE VARIATIONS DE HAUTEURS DE PLOTS : 144 – 207 – 270 ET 333 mm.

Plots laqués noir ou aluminités.

Modèles déposés.

EDITION STEPH SIMON 145, Boulevard Saint Germain – PARIS.6è –ODE.74-75

BIBLIOTHEQUE
RANGEMENT
CHARLOTTE
PERRIAND

COMPOSÉE PAR DES ÉLÉMENTS JOUES ET FONDS EN TOLE LAQUÉE AU FOUR ENTRETOISANT DES ETAGÈRES EN LATTE PLAQUÉ D'ESSENCES VARIÉES — PORTES COULISSANTES EN MÉTAL LAQUÉ, VERRE OU PLASTIQUE. JOUES PERFORÉES POUR L'ACCROCHAGE DE GLISSIÈRES PERMETTANT L'ADDITION D'ETAGÈRES INTERMÉDIAIRES EN GLACE OU DE COULISSER DES TABLETTES A DISQUES OU DES TIROIRS PLASTIQUES NORMES DE PROFONDEURS CONFORMES AUX ENCOMBREMENTS DES CLASSEMENTS VERTICAUX DE DISQUES OU DOCUMENTS COMMERCIAUX. POSSIBILITE DE CINQ HAUTEURS DE JOUES : 144 – 207 – 270 – 333 ET 522 mm. ET DE TROIS PROFONDEURS: 375 ET 420 mm. POUR SOLUTION MURALE– 480 POUR SOLUTION EN ÉPI.

a)- Etagères
b)- Joues perforées
c)- Tiges d'assemblage
d)- Equerre de fixation murale
e)- Portes coulissantes
f)- Tiroirs à glissières

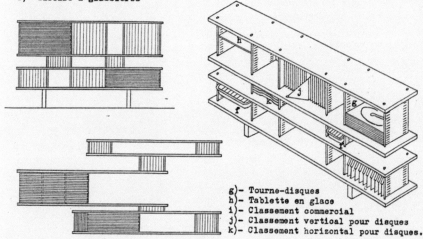

g)- Tourne-disques
h)- Tablette en glace
i)- Classement commercial
j)- Classement vertical pour disques
k)- Classement horizontal pour disques.

Modèles déposés.

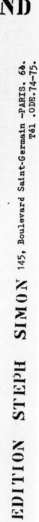

EDITION STEPH SIMON 145, Boulevard Saint-Germain –PARIS. 6è. Tél .ODE.74-75.

Perriand made technical drawings to manufacture her bookcase modules and accompanying parts. These brochures, produced by Galerie Steph Simon, demonstrate the different ways in which this kit of parts could be assembled.

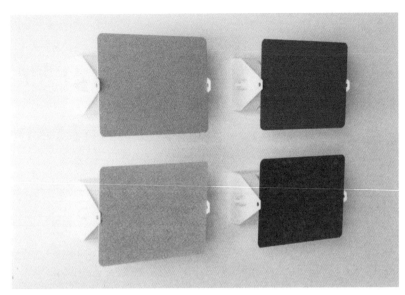

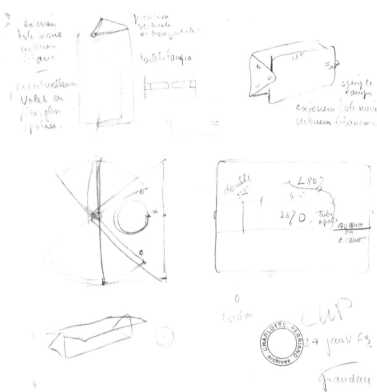

above   *Applique a volet pivotant* (Wall lights with adjustable shade), 1962
below   Sketch of the *Applique a volet pivotant*, 24 January 1963

Perriand designed many lights for her interiors during her career. She worked closely with Jean Prouvé to produce metal fittings for her designs. These wall-mounted shutter lights are adjustable so as to direct light where it is needed, and come in a range of colours. They can be installed individually to light a specific spot or in clusters to make a display.

Charlotte Perriand, Le Corbusier, Wardrobe for Pavillon du Brésil, 1956–9

This wardrobe was designed for use in Le Corbusier's housing project for Brazilian students in Paris. It works as a large room-dividing unit and uses Perriand's combination of industrial elements – plastic drawers and metal doors – within a wooden framework. There were ninety-two smaller units made, but only five at this larger scale. This was the last project on which Perriand and Le Corbusier collaborated.

1. Me Kraemer Bach. 2. Mme Catroux. 3. Mme Bidault. 4. Mme Harlette Gregh. 5. Nora Auric.
Schreiber-Crémieux. 9. Mme Simone Gaumont-Lanvin. 10. Françoise Giroud. 11. Simone Berria
Moreau. 15. Charlotte Perriand. 16. Colette Mars. 17. Renée-Pierre Gosset. 18. Rachel Dorange. 19. M

Frédérique Orvan, 'With a thousand apologies to the incumbent ministers, *Elle* constitutes
the first Ministry of Women', photomontage, published in *Elle* magazine, October 1950

Dornès. **7.** *Paule Corday.* **8.** *Suzanne*
nche Montel. **13.** *Carven.* **14.** *Mady*
20. *Suzy Solidor.* **21.** *Alix d'Unienville.*

In the years after the Second World War, France was in reconstruction mode – so efficient, modular construction was a priority. In light of this, in October 1950, *Elle* magazine presented 'as a laugh and with a thousand apologies', a fictional ministerial cabinet made up entirely of women. Perriand was appointed by *Elle* to the Ministry of Reconstruction. When asked what her programme would be, she spoke of the urgency of building housing, schools and hospitals, as well as introducing fixed rents for landlords and renter's rights for tenants. In the above photograph, Perriand is number 15.

Air France London agency, 1957. Medium-haul area located at the entrance;
on the left, Boomerang bench; on the right, ticket sales

Perriand had a long-standing relationship with the airline Air France, designing a number of its agencies and apartments around the world. In London, Perriand was appointed to refurbish a difficult site on New Bond Street after several other architects had failed to impress. The centrepiece of her design was a floor-to-ceiling bookcase. This was placed alongside a giant image of a Cambodian sculpture, intended to give customers the travel bug. Agents' desks were arranged in a saw-tooth pattern to give each customer their own space, while chairs by Charles and Ray Eames acted as points of colour.

above   Air France London agency, 1957. Long-haul bookings area,
         showing Perriand's room divider
below   Air France London agency facade, 1957

above   Air France London agency, 1957. Long-haul bookings area at Air France London,
showing Perriand's room divider
right   Drawing for Air France London shelving wall, 1957

35

above   Drawing for Air France London shelving wall and storage chest, 1957
below   Drawing for Air France London shelving wall, 1957

Ernő Goldfinger, Charlotte Perriand, illustration for the invitation
to the inauguration of French Railways House, London, 1963

Ernő Goldfinger, Charlotte Perriand, Reception desk at French Railways House, London, 1963

Londres, le 31 janvier 1967

Madame Charlotte Perriand,
18 rue las Cases,
Paris 7ᵉ

Ma chère Charlótte,

        Veux-tu trouver, ci-inclus, une
copie des dessins que j'ai emporté avec
moi à Londres.

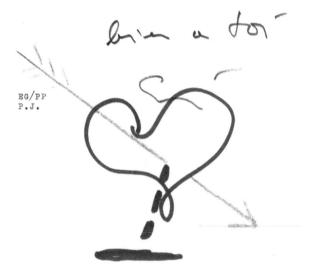

EG/PP
P.J.

Letter from Ernő Goldfinger to Charlotte Perriand, 1967

The celebrated architect Ernő Goldfinger invited Perriand to work with him on the interior of French Railways House on Piccadilly, London. The building had been designed by another London architecture practice, Shaw & Lloyd. Goldfinger and Perriand would also collaborate on the Paris office in 1967. Note the flirtatious way in which the two designers corresponded. Here, a simple note from Goldfinger to say that he is attaching some drawings of the Paris office comes with a doodle of a bleeding heart.

jane hall

the architecture of mass tourism

previous Charlotte Perriand, Pierre Jeanneret, recreation of the Refuge Tonneau, 1938 (original)
above   Charlotte Perriand, André Tournon (engineer), Bivouac refuge, Mont Joly, 1938

That was done by some old lady
who worked with a geezer called
Le Tordusier.[1]

Charlotte Perriand's work in the French Alps
came about in many ways simply because
she was there so often. Although her early
life, before the Second World War, was largely
spent in Paris, her love of the mountains is
palpable in her anecdotes and retellings
of the period, from weekend hikes to more
sustained moments both holidaying but also
building at altitude.[2] Perriand's first designs
for buildings, independent of Le Corbusier's
studio, were proposals for holidaying in
rural locations, and were entries for a set
of competitions organised in 1934 by the
magazine L'Architecture d'aujourd'hui
(The Architecture of Today).[3] Perriand
writes of how her 'hobby of canoeing'
inspired her entry for the first, a portable
weekend house on a riverbank.[4] Her scheme,
Maison de Week-end (Weekend House,
1934), which won her second place, was
a timber structure on stone pilings that
enclosed an open-air space 'complete with
barbecue'. Intended to 'blend in' with the
natural environment, the house came with
a diving board to encourage occupants to
'take a daily dip'.[5]

The design arranged two single-storey
volumes around a terrace, described by
Perriand as the 'true campsite of the house'
and conceived of as a room of its own. At the
centre of the plan, this outdoor 'room' would
be decorated by found objects from nature,
brought in by its occupants.[6] A number of
sketches for Maison au bord de l'eau (House
by the water) (1935), a slightly refined version
of Maison de Week-end, illustrates the terrace
as a covered space, with voids cut in the
tent-like roof to frame the sky, and tree trunks
employed as low seats around a table with
views out to the sea.[7] Perriand's furniture
for these designs was probably inspired by
her own collection of natural objects, which
she would forage for, sort and meticulously
photograph to form abstract and scaleless
sculptures she deemed her own form of
Art Brut.[8]

While Perriand's later work designing ski
resorts would concern the placement of
people within nature, her early building and
furniture projects of the 1930s brought nature
into the home in the form of these natural
objects, but also, among other designs, her
Straw Chair (1935) and 'free-form' furniture
(1938) made from solid pine.[9] The natural
materials used in both projects demonstrate

a clear divergence from more than a decade advocating tubular steel, the material of 'the Machine Age', with these organic forms at odds with the symmetry and order of the Modern Movement.

In her much quoted mini-manifesto 'Wood or Metal?' (1929), Perriand had presented materiality as a metaphor for both physical and mental health, describing wood as 'a vegetable substance, in its very nature bound to decay'. Metal on the other hand was elevated, 'play[ing] the same part in furniture as cement has done in architecture'.[10] As such, her early rejection of wood was not so much because of its material properties as for what it represented. She wrote, 'I was not interested in timber ... it didn't fit my ethic.'[11]

By 1935, however, Perriand had fully repudiated her position on natural materials, influenced by a greater interest in the way things are made, in part inspired by her experience of the mountains where she observed shepherds making seats from bits of wood, 'anything that came to hand'; their use of materials was a reflection of need, tied to a way of life.[12] While Perriand's material palette had changed, her reasons for choosing one material over another had not. Materiality did not simply denote what a design was made from but was an indicator of a way of living, part of an evolving 'ethic'. This coincided with a broader ideological shift that rejected leisure as an activity in binary opposition to work, regarding it instead as a descriptor for a way of being in the world.

work is leisure

L'Architecture d'aujourd'hui instigated its competitions in response to an emerging leisure society, which marginally pre-dated the recently elected Socialist government's 1936 policy to mandate paid holidays for all workers, but also the Modern Movement's concern for mass tourism.[13] In 1937, the Congrès international d'architecture moderne (CIAM) announced the natural landscape as the focus of its fifth meeting in Paris.[14]

Titled Logis et loisirs (Dwelling and Leisure), the conference presented the countryside not as anti-modern, but as an extension of the city, requiring a similar level of infrastructure to accommodate, as Josep Lluís Sert, chair of the conference, put it, '[the] great masses'.[15]

In this way, the reconstruction of the rural through the lens of modernity inextricably linked the city to the natural landscape. As a result, Perriand believed the former should benefit from 'air, sunshine, vegetation under-foot' and the latter from 'hygiene, technical and cultural progress', using the word 'leisure' to characterise a new reciprocity between 'material and spiritual well-being in both places'.[16] She shared with Le Corbusier, who had given the conference its theme, the view that leisure concerned not simply mass tourism to newly conceived 'extra-urban' locations, but the issue of millions of workers and their families' acquisition of a greater number of hours of free time in their everyday lives.[17] Perriand's biographer, Jacques Barsac, points out that while she agreed with his urgency to 'organise' leisure, she disagreed with his idea that it too should form a disciplined function. Rather, it was paramount that 'organisation' meant limiting the exploitation of the country-side by increased numbers of people.[18]

Perriand's work on the minimum dwelling, produced while at Le Corbusier's atelier, proved formative in thinking about new ways to locate people in the countryside. The Maison Loucher (1928), a 14-square-metre (150-square-foot) module 'adapted to industrialisation', was designed to provide the maximum in quality and space for the least expense; its compact nature was intended for high-density urban locations on a mass-produced scale. Released from the spatial constraints of urban density, however, prefabrication for a mountain site meant reducing the dwelling footprint but also creating schemes that were transportable to hard-to-access locations.[19]

As part of her rethinking of the Maison Loucher for greater Alpine exploration,

seriously began designing for mass tourism, working in collaboration with her long-term friend, the engineer Jean Prouvé, alongside architects Candilis, Josic and Woods on the design of three winter resorts in the valley of Belleville (1962).[26] Belleville was based on a previous competition entry Perriand designed while at Le Corbusier's studio, which nestled a building into a sloping site with its flat roof connecting to a pedestrian circulation zone.[27] The architecture of Belleville, designed for 25,000 people, would similarly be integrated with the mountain site so as to reduce its impact, while emphasising nature from within the building.[28]

Perriand addressed buildability in a handful of small structures she designed during this period. The first, the Bivouac Refuge (1937), designed with engineer André Tournon,[20] was made from a tubular-steel frame and walls in lightweight aluminium and hardboard sandwich panels.[21] A series of photos shows Perriand helping erect the structure, which took three days to assemble. Although temporary, the Bivouac remained on its Mont Joly site throughout the war.[22]

The second shelter, the Tonneau Refuge (1938), designed with Pierre Jeanneret, was a cylindrical structure similarly clad in aluminium and inspired by a fairground carousel the pair had seen while travelling in Croatia.[23] An improvement on the Bivouac, its shape resisted the snow and allowed for sleeping mats to be arranged concentrically, making it scalable for up to thirty occupants over several levels.[24] The ingenuity of these small designs was of modest impact, however, with neither mass-produced – an architecture limited to serious hikers and mountain climbers like Perriand herself.[25]

living leisure

Like her early furniture, the refuges required wealthy and informed patronage from those who could afford access to the mountains. It was not until Perriand's return from wartime years spent in Japan and Indochina that she

Eschewing the traditional pitched roofs of the local vernacular, the design used the apartment as a simulacrum for 'home', effectively privatising the natural setting through the transposition of the dwelling module on to a mountain location. However, with the building conceived as part of that same landscape, it formed a new type of public realm that prioritised equal access to views of the mountain through large communal terraces. Generated by the adjacent dwelling units, each had a pivoting wall that allowed the private space of the home to be made collective through its simple rotation.[29]

Towards the end of the decade, Perriand went on to develop many of these same design details for a number of buildings at Les Arcs, a ski resort in the Savoie region.[30] Attracted by the possibility of combining cultural and sporting activities, Perriand was in her sixties when she joined an already established team, whom she led to radically redesign the resort.[31] One of Perriand's most remarkable buildings was La Cascade at Arc 1600.[32] As at Belleville, Perriand suggested that the building should be laid out horizontally across the slope, with all the levels integrated within the hillside, which maintained the same size floorplan for each.[33] She used sugar cubes placed horizontally on a scaled version of the incline to show how the building would 'cascade' down the mountain.[34] The design cleverly

Charlotte Perriand and two friends during the installation of the Bivouac refuge, 1936–7

responded to changeable weather conditions: the southern terraces of La Cascade were arranged so as not to cast shadow on one another, and the northern facade was similarly realigned to prevent snow from reaching the ground-floor passageway. Like the majority of buildings at Les Arcs, La Cascade was built as a concrete frame, on Prouvé's suggestion, using hollow form-work to provide sound insulation.[35]

Perriand utilised designs developed over the course of her career to fit out the apartments in the buildings across Les Arcs, installing built-in storage units, which combined locally made furnishings with designs such as her Straw Chair (1935).[36] She designed fitted open-plan kitchens so that women were better connected to the rest of the family during their holidays (the assumption was, nevertheless, that they would still be the ones in the kitchen).[37] Not everybody appreciated the ingenuity of her designs, with Perriand 'dragging' some prospective apartment owners back to the resort to show them how all of her fixtures and fittings could in fact serve their needs.[38] From designer to saleswoman, Perriand worked tirelessly to demonstrate a new way of living, oriented towards the communal spaces with the mountain a shared amenity.

happy city dwellers

As France's skiing population rapidly grew in the post-war period, the mountains were no longer the preserve of a wealthy few, but open to every French person in search of a ski holiday.[39] In designing destinations for leisure activities, Perriand had hoped to keep the majority of the landscape in fact untouched, and was conflicted about creating what she later stated she hated most: 'organised leisure activities in these new mountain resorts'.[40] Leisure had come to be understood as a break from everyday routine – a reframing of the world that connected the urban dweller to the natural environment – yet for Perriand this way of living was very much the everyday ideal, the city and countryside interchangeable; the cows, birds and squirrels of Les Arcs were described, in her words, as 'happy city dwellers'.[41]

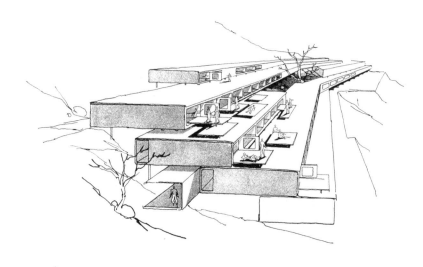

Georges Candilis, Alexis Josic, Charlotte Perriand, Henri Piot, Jean Prouvé, Ren Suzuki, Shadrach Woods, Competition for the development of a winter-sports resort in Belleville Valley, 1962. Perspective drawing showing the principle of cells extended by terraces arranged in tiers on the slope

Like them, she lived on site, designing, testing, building, walking, hiking, picking mushrooms – this way of life was formative in framing Perriand's relationship to the mountain site she was designing for.

Roger Godino, the developer of Les Arcs with whom Perriand had a protracted designer-client relationship, perceived this as the future of the leisure society, where holidays were not so much a break from work but the majority pastime of a 'new civilisation in which non-working activities will play a vital role'.[42] Perriand wrote to Godino lamenting their achievements at Les Arcs, but also agreeing with his point – less in response to the economic future he predicted, but as an ideal, highlighting societies in Southeast Asia where 'they do not consume leisure, they live it'.[43] In 1996, Perriand rebuked the curators of the Design Museum's last retrospective of her work for portraying her solely as a furniture designer.[44] While her own phrase 'from concrete to spoon' summarises the breadth of her design approach, it still doesn't quite capture what she achieved in the mountains, and the way in which she *lived* her designs with others.[45]

Charlotte Perriand, Gaston Regairaz, Mockup of the site plan for Arc 1600, 5 November 1967

Charlotte Perriand, Gaston Regairaz, La Cascade residence at Arc 1600, 1967–9. Les Arcs presentation photograph

1   Tourist at Les Arcs quoted by Perriand in her autobiography: *Charlotte Perriand, A Life of Creation* (New York: Monacelli Press, 2003), 321.

2   Jacques Barsac, Sébastien Cherruet and Pernette Perriand (eds), *Charlotte Perriand: Inventing a New World* (Paris: Foundation Louis Vuitton and Gallimard, 2019), 125.

3   Perriand (2003), 81.

4   Ibid.

5   Ibid.

6   Starlight Vattano and Giorgia Gaeta, 'The Minimum House Designs of Pioneer Modernists Eileen Gray and Charlotte Perriand', *Athens Journal of Architecture*, 2/2 (2016), 162.

7   Charlotte Perriand, *Maison au bord de l'eau*, 1934, featured in Barsac, Cherruet and Perriand (2019), 146.

8   Perriand (2003), 97.

9   Barsac, Cherruet and Perriand (2019), 122.

10 Charlotte Perriand, 'Wood or Metal?', *The Studio*, 97 (April 1929), 278–79.

11 Martin Meade and Charlotte Ellis, 'Interview with Charlotte Perriand', *Architectural Review*, 1053 (November 1984), www.architectural-review.com/essays/interview-with-charlotte-perriand [Accessed 9 August 2020].

12 Ibid.

13 Tom Avermaete, 'Travelling Notions of Public and Private: The French Mass Tourism Projects of Candilis – Josic – Woods', *OASE*, 64 (2004), 22.

14 CIAM 5 was held in Paris 28 June–2 July 1937. Perriand in fact left Le Corbusier's atelier in 1937 over a disagreement concerning the organisation of the conference, because Le Corbusier had rejected the inclusion of a younger generation of Marxist architects, despite utilising their free labour to enable the conference to happen. Charlotte Perriand, who advocated for this group, left Le Corbusier's atelier as a result. See Rixt Hoekstra, 'Women and Power in the History of Modern Architecture: The Case of the CIAM Women', in *MoMoWo: Women Designers, Craftswomen, Architects and Engineers between 1918 and 1945*, ed. Caterina Franchini, Helena Seražin and Emilia Maria Garda (Ljubljana: ZRC Publishing House, 2017). See also Annie Pedret, *Team 10: An Archival History* (London: Routledge, 2013), 45.

15 Avermaete (2004), 16.

16 Jacques Barsac, *Charlotte Perriand: Complete Works, Volume 1, 1903–1940* (Zurich: Scheidegger & Spiess, 2014), 92. Emphasis added.

17 Barsac, Cherruet and Perriand (2019), 130.

18 Ibid.

19 Claire Grangé, 'The Art of Mountain Living', *ARCHALP*, 3 (2019), 28.

20 Tournon was an engineer at Aluminium Français and had previously participated in the design of the failed Vallot hut, a timber structure that had to be pulled up (with difficulty) to its windy 4,000-metre site on Mont Blanc. Perriand (2003), 92.

21 The Bivouac refuge was first constructed on the banks of the Seine in Paris, and then on Saint-Nicolas de Véroce in the Haute-Savoie. Barsac (2014), 320.

22 Mary McLeod (ed.), *Charlotte Perriand: An Art of Living* (New York: Harry N. Abrams, 2003), 184.

23 Barsac, Cherruet and Perriand (2019), 148.

24 Ibid., 133.

25 Perriand has been described as a very skilled sportswoman, who skied until the age of seventy-five.

Pierre Blanc, who was known locally as 'The Pope', introduced her to mountain climbing in the 1920s. See Jacques Barsac, *Charlotte Perriand: Complete Works, Volume 4, 1968–1999* (Zurich: Scheidegger & Spiess, 2019), 25.

26 It was during this period, in 1960, that Perriand built herself a small cabin in Méribel-les-Allues. Carmen Espegel, *Women Architects in the Modern Movement* (London: Routledge, 2018), 229. Candilis, Josic and Woods had long been interested in the impact of leisure on the daily lives of mass society, particularly in the relationship between France's emerging welfare society and mass consumption. Over the course of twenty-four years, they designed more than ninety projects for tourism. See Avermaete (2004), 16.

27 The competition entry was designed by Perriand, Jeanneret and Le Corbusier in 1938 for a site in Vars in the Queyras Mountains. See Perriand (2003), 327.

28 Barsac, Cherruet and Perriand (2019), 125.

29 Perriand constructed a similar rotating facade for her project Le Vieux Matelot, the refurbishment of a small building twenty-six years prior to Belleville's design. See Avermaete (2004), 32.

30 Perriand came to the attention of Roger Godino, the developer of Les Arcs, through her editorship of an issue of *L'Architecture d'aujourd'hui* titled 'Building Large Mountain Resorts'. He also visited the small chalet she designed and built in Méribel. See Perriand (2003), 313.

31 Ibid. Les Arcs is formed by a series of resorts each named after their altitude: Arc 1600, 1800, 2000. See India Block, 'Charlotte Perriand's Les Arcs ski resort celebrates 50 years', *Dezeen* (12 July 2019), www.dezeen.com/2019/07/12/les-arcs-architecture-charlotte-perriand-50-years [Accessed 9 August 2020].

32 La Cascade replaced the design for three towers by the firm AAM.

33 Perriand (2003), 316.

34 Barsac (2019), 43.

35 Perriand (2003), 316.

36 Now produced by Galerie Steph Simon in Paris. See Perriand (2003), 317.

37 The open-plan kitchens were based on her 1927 design for a project called *Travail et Sport*. Barsac (2019), 65. Mary Novakovich, 'An architectural ski tour: Les Arcs, 50 years on', *Guardian* (30 November 2019), www.theguardian.com/travel/2019/nov/30/skiing-les-arcs-an-architectural-ski-tour-50-years-anniversary-modernist [Accessed 9 August 2020].

38 Perriand even gave out her phone number to people who wanted to construct additional walls in their apartment, so that she could persuade them not to. See Perriand (2003), 322.

39 Godino, as quoted in ibid., 326.

40 Ibid., 379.

41 Ibid., 316.

42 In her autobiography, Perriand makes constant reference to the fact that she did not prioritise the economics of Les Arcs. She writes that she was scolded for this on a number of occasions by Godino, for whom managing costs came first, causing him 'anxiety for 15 years'. See Perriand (2003), 381.

43 Ibid., 380.

44 Ibid., 370.

45 Grangé (2019), 31.

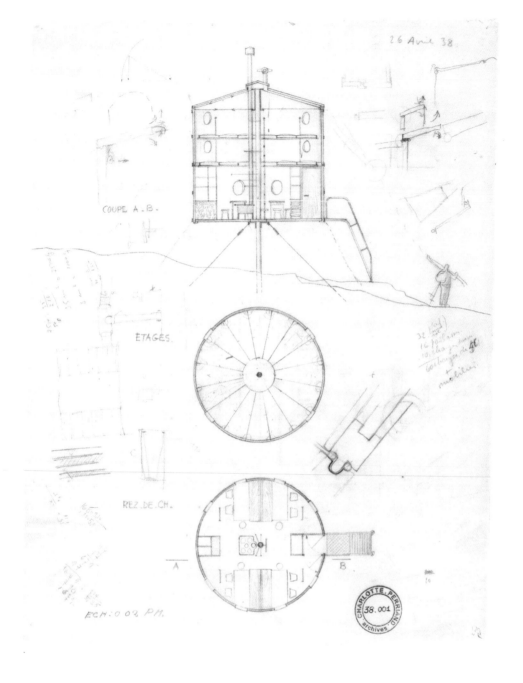

Charlotte Perriand, Pierre Jeanneret, Refuge Tonneau, December 1938. Cross-section sketch showing position of beds

Perriand found an unlikely source of inspiration for the design of her mountain refuge – a children's merry-go-round. This was translated into the futuristic-looking Refuge Tonneau. Consisting of a tubular-steel frame and twelve prefabricated aluminium panels, it could be erected in just four days. It was lightweight enough to be carried up steep slopes and robust enough to withstand extreme Alpine weather. Perriand, collaborating with Pierre Jeanneret, designed the interior to be compact and easily transformable. The beds can be used as benches during the day, while cubic stools provide storage.

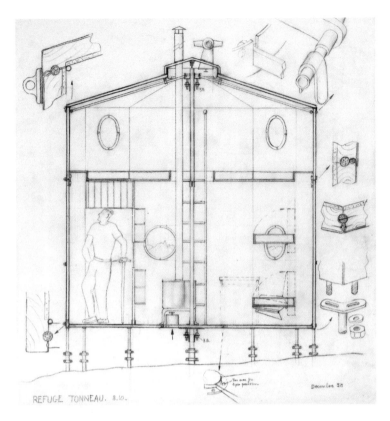

REFUGE TONNEAU. 8.10.

above   Charlotte Perriand, Pierre Jeanneret, Refuge Tonneau, December 1938. Cross-section sketch
below   Charlotte Perriand, Pierre Jeanneret, Refuge Tonneau model, 1938. Photograph with Perriand
         at the door and a friend sitting on a rock

Méribel chalet, 1960. Main room on the ground floor

Méribel chalet, closed bed, bay window and gable wall, 1960

Between 1960 and 1961, Perriand designed and built herself a small chalet in Méribel-les-Allues in France's Savoie region – not far from the ski resorts she would later design in the same area. In her autobiography, she wrote that it was the perfect space for daydreaming, where she would often escape when she needed a break from the city. Nestled on the side of a mountain overlooking a valley, the chalet has two floors that can be entered from the slope outside, and a large terrace. The interior is minimal, with wood and exposed stone. Perriand was inspired by the rustic furniture of Savoie, where her grandparents lived, while details such as straw *tatami* mats point to her years spent in Japan. The interior feels traditional but is highly modern.

above   Charlotte Perriand in front of the Méribel chalet under construction, 1960
below   Charlotte Perriand skiing in the mountains, 1938

Charlotte Perriand rock climbing, 1928

Charlotte Perriand facing a valley, c. 1930

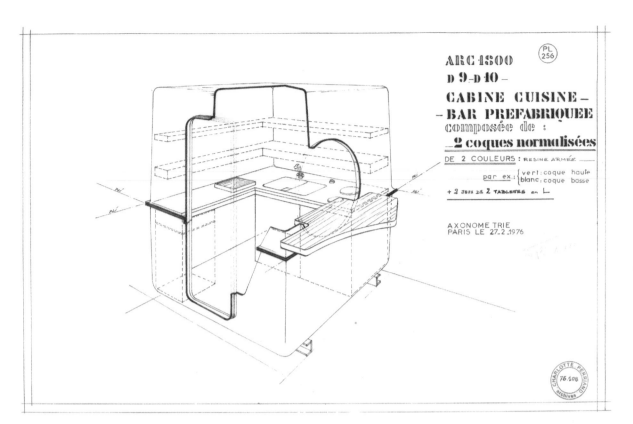

above   Axonometric drawing of the prefabricated kitchen–bar cubicle consisting of two
standardised shells for the Belles Challes-Lauzières residences, 27 February 1976
below   Prefabricated bathroom being installed by crane at Les Arcs, c. 1978
right   Prefabricated kitchen unit, 1975

From the start, Perriand wanted to prefabricate the kitchens and bathrooms for Les Arcs. Her idea was to use cranes to lift the ready-made modules into place, so as to avoid clashing with various trades (plumbers, painters, electricians, tilers) working in restricted spaces. Her idea was initially rejected, and it was only with the construction of Arc 1800 that prefabricated elements began to be used. The installation was undertaken by shipbuilders who were experienced in producing modular bathrooms and kitchens made of polyester fibre.

Pentagonal table with cross-shaped metallic leg assembly, May 1976.
Designed for the Lauzières residence, Arc 1800

Interior of the Lauzières residence at Arc 1800, 1976

Charlotte Perriand, Gaston Regairaz, Versant Sud complex, Arc 1600, 1969–75

Charlotte Perriand, Gaston Regairaz, Arc 1600, 1967–9. North facade of the Cascade residence

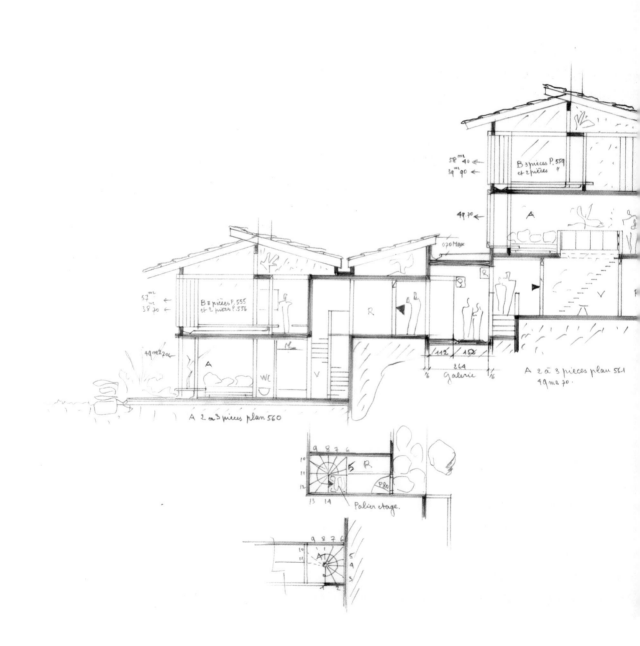

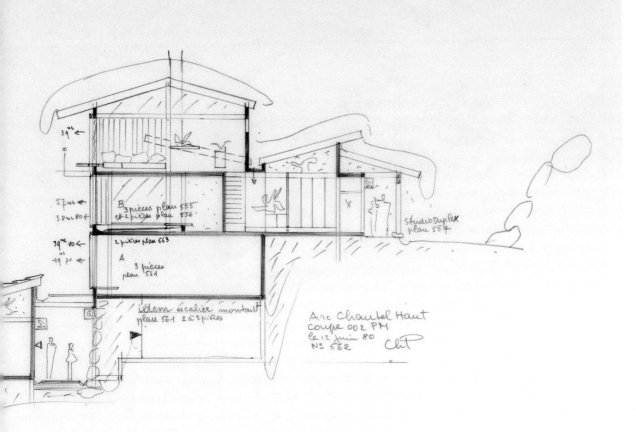

39 m2

57 m2
38 m2 80

39 m2 80
ou
49 70

B 3 pièces plan 555
et 2 pièces plan 556

2 pièces plan 563

A   3 pièces
plan 561

Studio Duplex
plan 557

idem escalier montant
plan 561 2 ou 3 pièces

Arc Chantel Haut
coupe 002 PM
le 12 Juin 80
N° 562   ChP

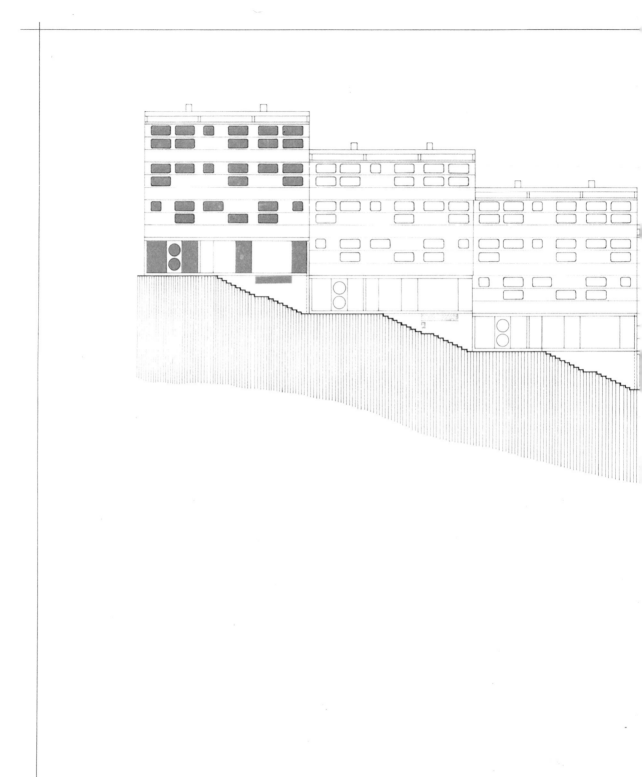

Elevation of the north facade of the Cascade residence, Arc 1600, 16 December 1968

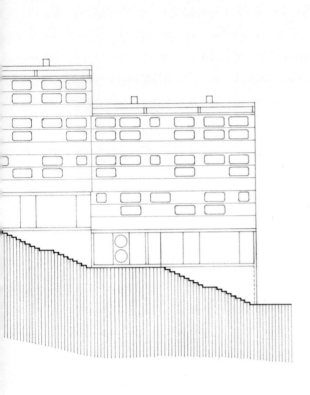

RECT 25 JAN'69

SAVOIE COMMUNE DE BOURG ST MAURICE
STATION DE L'ARC 1 600

IMMEUBLE B I		ELEVATION FACE NORD		C
CHP 15 rue Las cases PARIS VII	0.01	16 DEC'68	M.H	62

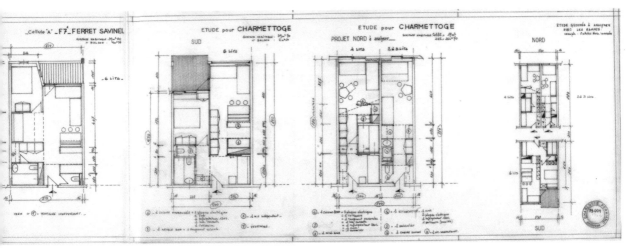

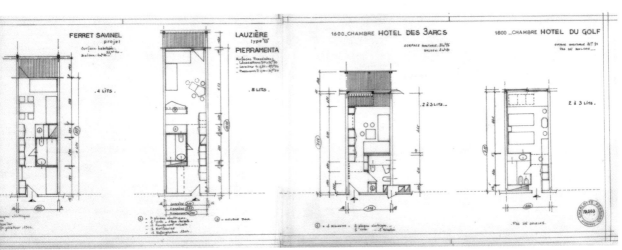

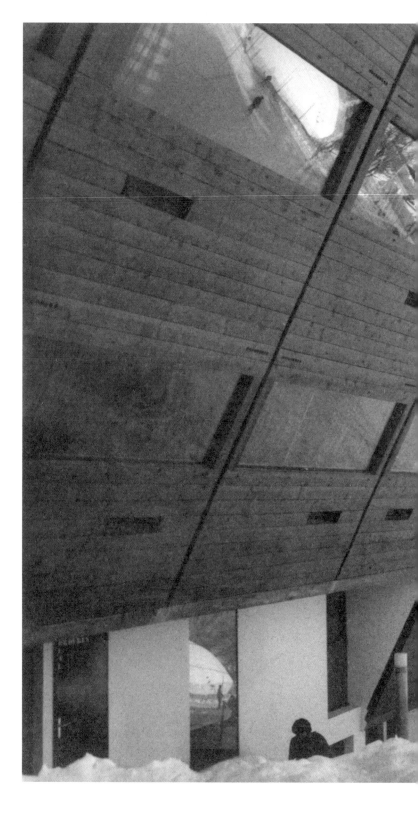

North facade of the Cascade residence, Arc 1600, 1967–9

Charlotte Perriand, Gaston Regairaz, Arc 1600, 1967–9. North facade of the
Cascade residence in the background and La Coupole in the foreground

Charlotte Perriand in her studio, Paris, January 1991

Charlotte Perriand at the Méribel chalet, c. 1984

acknowledgements

This book was published in conjunction with the exhibition
Charlotte Perriand: The Modern Life at the Design Museum,
London, 19 June to 5 September 2021.

Curator: Justin McGuirk
Assistant Curator: Esme Hawes
Associate Curators: Pernette Perriand, Jacques Barsac
and Sébastien Cherruet
Exhibition Project Manager: Cleo Stringer
Exhibition Project Coordinator: Jessica Taylor
Exhibition Design: Assemble
Exhibition Graphic Design: A Practice for Everyday Life
Reconstruction Content Partner: Cassina

The Design Museum owes its gratitude to all the lenders of the
exhibition. Special thanks to colleagues and friends who have
generously shared their knowledge and advice to aid the curatorial
development of the exhibition.

Thank you to Design Museum Benefactors and the Charlotte Perriand
Circle of Friends for their support of the exhibition: Anne Pierre
d'Albis-Ganem, Miel de Botton, Isabelle Hotimsky, Kathy Matsui,
Melissa Morris, John and María Pfeffer, Rafic Saïd

Publication Partner
CHRISTIE'S

biographies

Glenn Adamson is a curator, writer and historian based in New York. He has previously been Director of the Museum of Arts and Design, and Head of Research at the Victoria and Albert Museum. His publications include *The Craft Reader* (2010), *Postmodernism: Style and Subversion* (2011, co-edited with Jane Pavitt), *The Invention of Craft* (2013), *Art in the Making* (2016, co-authored with Julia Bryan-Wilson) and *Fewer Better Things: The Hidden Wisdom of Objects* (2018). Glenn was curator of *Beazley Designs of the Year 2017*, at the Design Museum, and is co-host of the online interview series Design in Dialogue. Glenn's newest book is *Craft: An American History* (2021).

Jacques Barsac is a writer, researcher and director of around forty documentaries on art and history. His films have won over twenty awards at international festivals, including, most notably, *Le Corbusier* (1987). He is the author of seven books on Perriand: *Charlotte Perriand, un art d'habiter* (2005), *Charlotte Perriand et le Japon* (2008), *Charlotte Perriand et la Photographie* (2011) and the four-volume catalogue raisonné *Charlotte Perriand: Complete Works* (2014–19). He was also the co-curator of the exhibitions *Charlotte Perriand et la photographie* at the Petit Palais (2011), *Charlotte Perriand et le Japon* at the Musée d'art moderne et contemporain (2013), and *Charlotte Perriand: Inventing a New World* at Fondation Louis Vuitton (2019).

Tim Benton is a leading researcher in Modernist architecture, with Le Corbusier as his special field of expertise. Benton has published a number of books, including a classic study of the design of Le Corbusier's villas in Paris in the 1920s (1984) that was republished in a revised edition as *The Villas of Le Corbusier and Pierre Jeanneret, 1920–1930* (2007). More recent publications include *The Rhetoric of Modernism: Le Corbusier as a Lecturer* (2009), *LC FOTO: Le Corbusier Secret Photographer* (2013) and *Le Corbusier, peintre à Cap-Martin* (2015). He also contributed to the exhibition *Charlotte Perriand* at the Pompidou Centre (2005).

Sébastien Cherruet is an art historian and head of institutional relations at the luxury conglomerate LVMH. He co-curated the exhibition *Charlotte Perriand: Inventing a New World* at Fondation Louis Vuitton in Paris (2019).

Jane Hall is the inaugural recipient of the British Council Lina Bo Bardi Fellowship (2013) and founding member of the London architecture collective Assemble, who won the Turner Prize in 2015. She completed a PhD at the Royal College of Art (2018), where her research looked at the legacy of modernist architects in both Brazil and the UK. Her particular focus is on interdisciplinary practice between artists and architects, and the emergence of alternative methods for architectural design. Jane is also the author of the book *Breaking Ground, Architecture by Women* (2019).

Tim Marlow is Chief Executive and Director of the Design Museum in London. Formerly Artistic Director of the Royal Academy of Arts and Director of Exhibitions at White Cube, Tim has been involved in the contemporary art world for the past thirty years as a curator, writer and broadcaster. He has worked with many of the most important and influential artists of our time to deliver wide-ranging and popular programmes, and brings a commitment to diverse and engaging exhibitions to his new role showcasing the transformational capability of design. Tim sits on the board of trustees for the Imperial War Museum, Sadler's Wells Theatre, Art on the Underground Advisory Board and Cultureshock Media. He was awarded an OBE in 2019.

Justin McGuirk is Chief Curator at the Design Museum. He has been the design critic of the *Guardian*, the editor of *Icon* magazine and the Head of Design Curating and Writing at Design Academy Eindhoven. He is the author of *Radical Cities: Across Latin America in Search of a New Architecture* (2014), and co-editor of *Fear and Love: Reactions to a Complex World* (2016), *California: Designing Freedom* (2017) and *Home Futures: Living in Yesterday's Tomorrow* (2018).

Penny Sparke is Professor of Design History at Kingston University and the Director of the Modern Interiors Research Centre. From 1999 to 2005, she was Dean of the Faculty of Art, Design and Music at Kingston University and from 2005 to 2014 she was Pro Vice-Chancellor for research and enterprise. She has given keynote addresses, curated exhibitions, and broadcast and published widely in the field of design history. Her most important publications include *Italian Design from 1860 to the Present* (1989), *As Long as It's Pink: The Sexual Politics of Taste* (1995), *Elsie de Wolfe: The Birth of Modern Interior Decoration* (2005), *The Modern Interior* (2008) and *Nature Inside: Plants and Flowers in the Modern Interior* (2021).

index

picture credits

Design Museum Publishing
Design Museum Enterprises Ltd
224–238 Kensington High Street
London W8 6AG
United Kingdom

designmuseum.org

First published in 2021
© 2024 Design Museum Publishing

ISBN 978-1-872005-52-2

Publishing Manager: Mark Cortes Favis
Junior Publishing Manager: Stefano Mancin
Assistant Editors: Giulia Morale and Esme Hawes
Picture Researchers: Esme Hawes and James McLean
Copyeditor: Simon Coppock
Proofreaders: Ian McDonald and Cecilia Tricker
Production Controller: Chris Benfield
Design: A Practice for Everyday Life

Many colleagues at the Design Museum have
supported this book, and thanks go to them all.

Distribution

UK, Europe and select territories around the world
Thames & Hudson
181A High Holborn
London WC1V 7QX
United Kingdom
thamesandhudson.com

USA and Canada
ARTBOOK | D.A.P.
75 Broad Street, Suite 630
New York, NY 10004
United States of America
artbook.com

Printed and bound in Belgium by Graphius